HELPING YOUR CHILD
Become...

BY TIM & KIRSTEN KING

Insignia
PUBLICATIONS

Insignia Publications
Sacramento, California

Helping Your Child Become...
By Tim & Kirsten King

© 2004 Tim & Kirsten King

Library of Congress Control Number 2004104545
ISBN 0-9748100-1-0

Printed in the United States of America
First publication July 2004

Photography by Jill Lewis & Bruce Robinson Studios
Cover Illustration by Matt Jones & Jason Weller (www.7DCreative.com)

Printing and design by Insignia Publications (www.insigniabooks.com)

To order additional copies or other publications visit us at:
www.HelpingYourChildBecome.com

Price $14.95

THIS BOOK IS LOVINGLY DEDICATED TO

ADAM
EMILY
TREVOR
MCKENZIE
NOAH

OUR PRAYER IS THAT WITH
GOD'S WISDOM AND GUIDANCE WE ARE

HELPING YOU
Become...

Acknowledgements and Thanks

This book does not come from perfection, but from striving. We in no way claim to have every answer on the subject of parenting. In fact, the more we learn, the more humble we feel. At this writing the oldest of our five children is 17 years-old and the youngest is 7. It is most certainly premature to call ourselves 'experts.' We are NOT experts, but specialists. We have not done things perfectly, but we are growing in understanding of God's perfect principles and strive to do them. Only look to us as we point to Jesus.

Our first thanks goes to those five individuals that motivated us to search out the truths that are in this book. God entrusted us with your precious lives to mold and shape. We are humbled and honored at the privilege, and pray that as you look back on your childhoods, you will see that we gave you our whole hearts and our best efforts. It is our chief desire that you rise above us in wisdom, talent and spirit. We want you to stand on our shoulders and reach for the stars. We are continually blessed by the people that you are becoming. You will do great things for Jesus! We love you Adam, Emily, Trevor, McKenzie and Noah! You are the best.

Of the many people whose lives have influenced us in our Christian walk, none have impacted us as deeply or profoundly as our own Pastor Nathaniel J. Wilson and his precious and powerful wife, Sister Mary Wilson. For nearly twenty years, the goal and motto of The Rock Church has been "Helping People Become…" The Wilson's have been the ultimate examples of this mission. They have unselfishly poured themselves into our lives, encouraging us to great heights when we felt only inches tall and telling us we would do great things when we had a difficult time believing it ourselves. They gave us vision and passion for our family. They baptized us, married us, taught us how to be sweethearts, dedicated our children to the Lord one by one, baptized them, prayed them through and pronounced blessings over them. They have showed us how to have a blast as a family and how to war for our children's hearts. They continue to shepherd our souls. It was Pastor Wilson's encouragement that led us to endeavor to write this book. He simply said, "Tim and Kirsten, you need to write a book. You have a lot to say; it is time you said it." He has been 'Daddy Wilson' to Tim for twenty-three years. Their belief in us and unwavering love is truly helping us to become... Thank you both for your love and support. You are a rock! We love you.

Thanks to those special people that we call family. Kirsten's parents, Terry and Dorothy Compton gave her the desire for excellence, a ready laugh, a love for music, and so much more. I look back with fondness to many childhood memories. Thank you. I love you both. Love and thanks to my sister, Dana Stansbery, with whom I never fought! Your friendship is a precious jewel. We love you and Dave, Madeline and Emma. To Uncle Cliff and Aunt Louise Carnes, who have been there so many times for us. For playing in the pool, sharing wheat crackers, care packages, baby sitting times five, and encouragement, encouragement, encouragement, we love you. Thanks would be incomplete without the mention of Tim's grandfather, Max Shipman Winter. Although you have gone on, Gramps, I pray that your practical wisdom lives on in me. When everything around me was chaotic and tumultuous, you were the calm in the storm. Your encouragement to go to college and rise above my circumstances was priceless. I will always love you, and miss you every day.

We must thank a few others whose examples and influence have truly made a mark on our growth as Christians and a family: Pastor Harold and Judy Sargent, Bob and Joanne Bertram, and Jim and Ruby Jones. Kirsten thanks her 'Mamas in the Lord': Mary Wilson, Judy Sargent, Joanne Bertram, Dorothy Newton, Ruby Jones, and Barbara English. You have prayed with and for me, answered my questions, listened to my concerns, and loved my children as your own. We are as one! I love you all!

Thank you to our comrades in the trenches for being faithful friends. Few people in life are as blessed as we are to have such a network of loving friends. We have diapered together, pulled baby teeth together, had play time together, taught lessons on life together, and are now seeing our oldest 'babies' drive off and enter college together. Wow! What a journey. Thank you for your friendship, your influence on our children, and your desire to raise Godly children yourselves. Pastor Myles and Sheila Young, Beth and David Ezell, Pastor Steve and Debbie Malone, Bob and Patti Felt, Ron and Julie Short, Pastor Gerry and Jenny Mallory, Gene and Jill Lewis, and Wayne and Paula Scott. What a grand adventure!

Thank you to the Rock Church family. You have encouraged and supported us, taught us and loved us. Thank you for helping us become.

Specific thanks to our editor Patricia Bollmann, who has added polish and clarity to this work, as well as given us timely encouragement. You are one brilliant, Godly lady! Thank you.

Our publisher Matt Jones is a craftsman. He has taken our raw ideas and created a perfect representation of what we wanted to portray. Thank you, 7D Creative and Insignia Press for helping us birth our "sixth child," this book.

What words can express what you mean to both of us, Beth. You have kept the dream alive when we would have given up on ourselves. You are the other half of Kirsten's brain, finishing her thoughts, being sensitive, discerning and encouraging. You are invaluable. No one is more blessed than we are to count you as a friend.

Our ideas and understandings of successful Biblical parenting have been shaped by a number of authors on the subject, Dr. James Dobson, Michael and Debi Pearl, Reb Bradley, Ted Tripp, Gary and Ann Marie Ezzo, Susan Shaufer McCaulley, Richard Fugate and many others. They have influenced our understanding of the importance and methods of Biblical child training. We have tried diligently to acknowledge their ideas throughout this book; so many of these thoughts, practices, and terms have become ingredients in the 'soup' of our philosophy. We are thankful to those whose passions have instructed us and ignited the fire of passion to search the scriptures ourselves, to lead our children in the old paths and minister to other hungry families.

"There is no limit to what a man can do or where he can go, if he doesn't care who gets the credit."
                                                                    - Ronald Reagan

Forward

One can read a book and deduce that it is well-written, well researched, and exceptionally insightful in equipping one for the particular challenges of life which the book addresses. The value of such a book is dependent only on the author's knowledge and scholarship, and has no necessary connection to his/her moral character or success with their own family.

However, when writing on subjects such as marriage and family, it is not unfair to look at the life of the author(s) as part of the criteria for judging the value and credibility of their work.

One who reads this book by Tim and Kirsten King will be immediately struck by the unusual insightfulness and understanding page after page. It is not another "pop" book on child-rearing, but rather a well-thought out and measured response to the needs of families today. The understanding revealed in regards to the notion of "training" alone is worth much more than the price of the book. An extra bonus is the writing skills and ability of expression found on every page.

However, none of the above qualifies as the most impressive thing about this book. For the most impressive thing about this book is the King family. Tim is an exemplary father with a miraculous and amazing testimony of his own. Kirsten is a model mother and very wise woman. Their children are lively, real, and have a genuine zest for life—yet are respectful, gracious, and manifest enviable self-restraint.

The girls are vibrant and beautiful. The boys are strong and masculine, yet fully aware of the place in life for respect, obedience, and gentility. All of them are committed to learning, and show an eagerness to take on the challenges of life. And, of course, without question, God, His will, and His purposes, are first in everything and in every way for the entire family.

This is one book you can read with the full awareness that the author's have tested it all in the crucible of real life—and the result is pure gold. This book comes with my highest recommendation.

Nathaniel J. Wilson

May 10, 2004

Contents

Part One
Helping your child become...Self-Controlled

Part Two
Helping your child become...Wise

Part Three
Helping your child become... Responsible

Chapter One

BLUEPRINT FOR SUCCESS

I am at my wits' end. I know that I yell too much. I want to do everything right, but I feel like such a failure." The young mother's eyes glistened with tears. For ten minutes she had poured out her frustrations, recounting how her two young children would run from her, laughing over their shoulders, in a wearisome game of catch-me-if-you-can. The young mother went on to express her frustration at her oldest daughter's habitual distraction from simple directions: "When I check to make sure she has done what I asked, she is either playing with her baby dolls or coloring a picture. I know she is smart enough to do the tasks. I really think she enjoys annoying me."

We smiled, because in the past we had experienced the same level of frustration.

Tim was brought up amid the chaos of alcoholism and drug abuse. His single mother gave him little or no supervision. She would often carouse for days, leaving Tim and his little brother alone. As Tim grew, so did his resentment, bitterness, and anger. After breaking his neck in a diving accident at the age of seventeen, Tim lay in the hospital faced with the possibility of life as a quadriplegic. In desperation Tim made a "deal" with God: "You let me walk away from this accident, and I will search until I find you." After two months of hospitalization and countless hours of physical therapy, Tim walked out of the hospital and kept his promise to God. He accepted a friend's invitation to a Bible study, and found the Lord in West Sacramento, California, in 1982, in a fledgling congregation of 25 led by young Pastor Nathaniel Wilson. Tim was twenty years old.

Kirsten was raised in a beautifully decorated home. Her parents were adamant about education, table manners, proper speech, and common courtesies. She had been groomed for "success," but her heart was empty. Even as a small child, she cried out to God. Longing to know Him and His love intimately, she searched for years to find His truth. Then through mutual friends and a series of small miracles, Tim and Kirsten were introduced. Being an eager, young Christian of two years, Tim invited Kirsten to the same church that had now grown to 75 members and were meeting in a warehouse in South Sacramento. She entered the sanctuary of God, found His beautiful people, and discovered living on a whole new plane.

After a brief courtship, we were married. We were two young people, with imperfect backgrounds and little preparation for the life that lay ahead of us. When we looked around us at our new brothers and sisters, we saw unity and joy in many of their families and homes. We marveled at the love of God these parents shared with their little ones. We noticed that some of the young people seemed far ahead of their worldly counterparts in graceful manner, leadership, maturity, talent, and focus. Oh, how we wished that we had received the training that these blessed young people had received! Their parents seemed so wise. We desired relationships like these with our eventual children. On the other hand, we were surprised to discover that even with the truth of God's Word and a godly heritage that spanned three and four generations, some of the grown children did not treasure their homes, families, and heritage. What was different about the way these children had been raised? Knowing that both of our backgrounds lacked godly, biblical training, we were at a loss as to how we would raise our children when the time came. However, we were determined that our children would experience what we had missed. That we would train our children in the house of the Lord and in His ways became our consuming desire.

> That we would train our children in the house of the Lord and in His ways became our consuming desire.

After our first child, Adam, entered our world, we eagerly approached a few of our "parenting heroes," hoping to unlock their secrets.

"Tell us, how did you raise such great children?" we asked, as we waited for the golden key of wisdom to be handed to us.

"My wife is just a good mom," said the loyal husband.

"Now, Honey, you are the best father. It comes so naturally to you," answered the humble mother.

"Okay, but *how* did you do it?" we asked hungrily. "What did you do along the way to raise such wonderful children who are now serving the Lord so sincerely?"

"Oh, we just relied on God. All the glory belongs to Him," they replied vaguely. Their responses made it seem as if good, godly parenting was done without any plan and that raising godly children just happened.

"Yes, of course. But what did you *do*?" we persisted, realizing that the task of nurturing children in the fear and admonition of the Lord does not just happen.

"Well, we just prayed. God did all the work," they chorused sweetly.

"Glory to God. But when they disobeyed, how did you discipline them? When they had a bad attitude, how did you correct them? When they didn't share, how did you teach them? How did they get such sweet, giving spirits? How did you foster their obvious love for the things of God? How did you encourage their talents and gifts so that they are now mightily used of God?" How...what...when...became our increasingly frustrated cry.

Aaaarrrrgh! We believed wholeheartedly that God was our ultimate teacher and guide, and that *all* glory for any good that would come out of our lives belonged to Him. However, we also knew that God had given us a complete guidebook to follow and that He used earthen vessels to accomplish His purposes. We were pretty sure that parents played a significant role in the development of good, godly kids. But we still didn't know what to *do*!

Apart from the success stories, we also observed some sad phenomena. Over the years, unfortunately, we saw many faithful parents lose their children to the world. We realized that even if a child is a second, third, or fourth generation Christian, it does not guarantee that he will grow up to be godly, wise, or responsible. In fact, a Christian heritage can provide a false sense of security that breeds a dangerous complacency. Many children who are raised "sleeping under the pews" turn from God in their adulthood, to the shock and sorrow of their parents. Other children never quite reach the full potential of their talents and gifts because their parents failed to instill the essential basic biblical training. The possible reasons for this failure are many: parental passivity, deferring training to the church, ignorance, misunderstanding the true nature of love, listening to secular "experts," or repeating their own parents' mistakes. However, the results are universal. These young adults struggle with faithfulness to God, to their job, to their spouse and children, and to financial stewardship.

> Good children don't just happen because they are raised in Godly homes.

Good children don't just *happen* because they are raised in Godly homes. So what are parents supposed to *do*?

We determined to read every Christian book that might hold some nuggets of parenting truth, beginning with the most powerful and authoritative, the Bible. We searched the Scriptures, attended seminars and Bible lessons, listened to tapes, and continued grilling those parents whose children exhibited the fruit we desired in our own children's lives. We avoided humanistic literature and godless parenting "experts." We were committed to discovering whatever we could from God's Word and His people that would help us do what had become a growing passion. We often wondered why we were so hungry to learn in this one area and why it had become such an intense purpose in our lives. We continually talked it, read it, and thought it.

Leading and guiding our little ones became our greatest joy, and it is now becoming our sweetest reward. No, we are *not* perfect parents; we are keenly and painfully aware of our humanness. But we feel like the lepers whose fortunes dramatically changed when they found a treasure: "We're not doing right. This is a day of good news and we are keeping it to ourselves…Let's report this…" (2 Kings 7:9 NIV).

God has given us a desire to share with you the

distillation of these years of focused study. It is our prayer that our years of frustrated searching, reading, and weeding will benefit you. If we can pass on to you some of the nuggets of wisdom that have been passed to us, we will feel successful. We want to give to you what we searched and begged for—what to *do* to raise godly children. Along with this parenting plan, we will provide the biblical support and reasoning behind it. It is our prayer that you, your family, and your church will be blessed by God's timeless principles of parenting.

The Misguided Builder

Imagine a builder beginning to nail boards together and saying, "You just watch (bam, bam, bam). When I'm finished, this is going to be a castle fit for a king (bam, bam, bam)."

"How many bedrooms will it have?" you ask curiously.

"Oh (bam, bam, bam), I'm not sure yet. We'll see what happens," he casually replies.

"Where are the living room and kitchen going to be?" you further question.

"Well, I was thinking they may go over here," he gestures in a general direction, "but we decided to just start in (bam, bam, bam) and see where we feel they should go as we get further in the process (bam, bam, bam)."

"Hmm, I see," you muse, thinking to yourself that this will be an interesting project to observe.

This poor, misguided builder has it all wrong. He has picked up his tools without envisioning his finished product, without formulating a plan to accomplish the project, or without making sure that his ideas satisfy the building codes. Without a doubt, his scheme will end in disaster, a waste of time and material. Proverbs 29:18 warns, " Where there is no vision, the people perish."

Before the foundation is poured, the builder should ask himself if he has a clearly defined vision of what the end product will look like. What elements should it contain? One story or two stories? How many bedrooms? Bathrooms? Separate family room, or kitchen/great room combination? One, two, or three-car garage? Although the eventual owner/occupant will infuse the individual touches that make the house a home, the builder must have a comprehensive design before he pounds the first nail. He cannot build on feelings alone.

Measure Twice, Cut Once
– the experienced carpenter's proverb

Similarly, imagine being overcome by a sweet urge to make a delicious treat. You throw a little sugar in the bowl. You rustle through the cupboards. Here are some marshmallows; toss in a few handfuls. What else… chocolate chips, corn syrup, and chocolate sauce all go haphazardly into the bowl. The resulting "delicious treat" becomes a culinary disaster because you failed to first identify what the finished product would be. Were you making red velvet cake or chocolate delight? Some of the most decadent recipes call for ingredients that are not at all appetizing if they are eaten separately. Think of flour, raw eggs, baking soda, and salt; none of these are sweet alone, but when measured correctly and mixed together with sugar, they become delicacies that tempt even the strongest will!

The Blueprint

Just as a reputable builder follows a detailed set of blueprints and specifications or just as a great chef follows a recipe, we must follow the blueprint and plans the Lord has given us for the raising of our children. The Bible is filled with instructions, admonitions, and warnings for parents to follow if they want their children to be successful, productive lovers of God. Parents cannot idle away their children's younger years without any planning and expect to see good results. It is not enough to take them to Sunday school, dress them in designer clothes, or expose them to classical music and great literature. Parenting takes much more vision, forethought, planning, and preparation than building a tri-level house or baking a seven-layer cake!

> Except the Lord build the house, they labour in vain that build it.
>
> Psalm 127:1

Thankfully, God, in His mercy, provided a flawless blueprint for life. It not only points the way to salvation and eternal life with Him, it gives comprehensive instruction in all facets of godly living, including the monumental task of child rearing. Ephesians 6:4 (NIV) summarizes the entire goal of parenting in one short, foundational verse: "Fathers, do not exasperate your children; instead, bring them up in the training and instruction of the Lord."

Let's expand some key elements of this Scripture because it provides the framework for this book. The word, *fathers,* appears to place the responsibility for child rearing squarely on Daddy's shoulders, letting Mama off the hook. Yet this is not so. (Did we just hear a collective baritone sigh of relief?) The Greek word for *fathers* is *pater,* or plural, *pateres,* which means "fathers," or, more correctly, "father and mother." Thus it is the shared duty of both parents to train up their children in the way they should go. As every married couple has discovered, God made man and woman different (understatement intended). Alone we are incomplete or imbalanced.

Together we are a complete construction team with the perfect blend of velvet and steel. The involvement of both parents is vital in the child rearing process.

It is true that not all homes are blessed with two parents who are in harmony, or even two parents at all. There are obvious advantages to having both parents united in the home, nevertheless the child of the single parent has special promises in the Word of God. Psalm 27:10 promises, "When my father and mother forsake me, then the Lord will take me up." God, himself, will take up the slack for the absent parent! Therefore, biblical principles apply to the single-parent home as well as to the two-parent home. We have personally seen many single mothers and fathers apply biblical child training principles, and they have brought peace to previously confused and chaotic situations.

The next critical element of Ephesians 6:4 is the charge to *bring them up.* The Greek word translated "*bring them up*" is defined, "to rear them up to maturity; to cherish or train, bring up, nourish." What is maturity? Webster's Dictionary offers a succinct definition: "the state of full development, perfected, worked out, or ready." Webster defines *training* as "guiding the mental, moral or spiritual development of another." Similarly, *instruction* means "to teach, educate, or inform." Our spiritual, moral, and mental training goals contain many vital characteristics: hungering after the Word of God, and being tender hearted, mannerly, diligent, hard working, persevering, "others minded," etc. These attributes cannot simply be hoped for; they must all be measured and planned for as the foundation is poured and framework is built in our children's lives. Are you beginning to get a clearer view of what the finished project should look like? The goal of parenting is to nurture our children to a state of full development or readiness for adult life through godly intellectual, practical, moral, and spiritual training.

Wow! What an undertaking. Where do we begin? What do we do? It seems as monumental a task as the old adage about eating an elephant, except eating the elephant doesn't take as much thought as it does time and persistence. The task of parenting is much more complex, albeit just as enormous, as eating the proverbial pachyderm. Successful parenting requires a strategy. After a broad study of the Old Testament and a concentrated study of the Book of Proverbs, Reb Bradley concludes that maturity is characterized by three major virtues: self-control, wisdom, and responsibility.[2] Our own study, along with supporting evidence, corroborates this conclusion. We have ordered our parenting strategy into these three broad categories of training and instruction: self-control, wisdom, and responsibility. Each aspect in the full scope of child training can be placed into one of these three areas.

Self-control is "not being governed by passions or emotions, craving, desires, wishes, or curiosity. It is the freedom from having to do what one feels like doing."[3] Self-control is being strong enough to say "no" to all selfish desires and to say "yes" to what is right. It is the ability to choose to do right in the face of temptation. This ability is basic to Christian living at any age and is the first area of focus in parenting. Success in the subsequent facets of child training hinges on achievement in this primary area.

Wisdom is knowledge rightly applied; it is using godly understanding and insight together with life experience to make sensible judgments and decisions. Wisdom requires acting with Christian character when no one is looking but God. Wisdom grows incrementally as we experience life. It is possible to embark upon instruction in wisdom with our children before they are completely self-controlled, but true wisdom requires growing self-government.

Responsibility involves "accepting personal accountability for one's own actions, as well as faithful and conscientious work habits, such as integrity, diligence, and reliability."[4] These characteristics are possible only when we are self-controlled and not ruled by passions.

Having introduced the blueprint and foundation for godly child training, let us go back to our hapless builder. He is nervously holding his breath as the building inspector tours the newly completed house. He is hoping that the inspector doesn't notice the obvious tilt of the foundation or that the walls aren't square. (He has spackled and textured the gaps between the walls and the ceiling so that the imperfections are less noticeable.) The builder's greatest fear is that the inspector will flip on the lights or flush the malfunctioning toilet. Oh, how he wishes now that he had followed a blueprint. What he had thought was a simple job was actually one that required much planning.

Unlike the builder, our vision is clear and the blueprint is true. We envision our children in a full state of development, ready for life. We are confident that with consistency and biblical help, we can successfully nurture them. The blueprint is godly intellectual, moral, practical, and spiritual training.

> Investing is simple, but not easy.
> – Warren Buffet

Simple, but Not Easy

It is our desire to give an answer to those parents who now ask, "What do we *do*?" Do not be misled; what is here proposed is not easy. Diligence, concentration and effort are required. Warren Buffet, the second wealthiest men in the world, made a profound statement regarding money: "Investing is simple, but not easy." Most people who are pursuing success in any arena think that the principles and steps that lead to great accomplishment must be complex and difficult. However, it is the little daily accomplishments that compound into great success. "For who hath despised the day of small things?" (Zech. 4:10). As you read this book, look for the simple and begin to implement the small things. We suggest that you read with a few highlighters in hand: pink for action items, yellow for ideas to ponder, etc. Use it as a guide. Mark it up. Write in the margins. As you implement the biblical principles, watch for positive changes in your family!

In the following chapters we will explore the biblical blueprint and the importance and interconnectedness of self-control, wisdom, and responsibility. We will give many practical examples and ideas for *helping your child become*...a delightful, productive, successful, and mature Christian.

Remember, It's simple....

- Good children don't just *happen* because they are raised in Godly homes.

- Just as any great chef follows a recipe or reputable builder has a thoroughly detailed set of blueprints and plans to follow in building a house, we must follow the blueprint and plans the Lord has given us for the raising of our children.

- The goal of parenting is to nurture our children to a state of full development or readiness for adult life through Godly intellectual, practical, moral, and spiritual training.

• Our parenting strategy falls into these three broad categories of training and instruction: self-control, wisdom, and responsibility.

Self-control is "not being governed by passions or emotions, craving, desires, wishes, or curiosity. It is the freedom from having to do what one feels like doing."

Wisdom is knowledge rightly applied; it is using Godly understanding and insight together with life experience to make sensible judgments and decisions.

Responsibility involves "accepting personal accountability for one's own actions, as well as faithful and conscientious work habits, such as integrity, diligence, and reliability."

• With consistency and Biblical help, we can accomplish our goal of nurturing our children to a full state of development or readiness for life through Godly intellectual, moral, practical and spiritual training.

• Be encouraged, it is the little daily accomplishments that compound into great success. It simply takes diligent, consistent and concentrated effort.

Chapter Two
MARRIAGE 101

*W*ait a minute! What is a chapter on marriage doing in a child-training book? The answer is, plenty. The optimal effectiveness of parenting and the ultimate success of children are directly tied to the strength of love and commitment in a marriage. The unity between spouses is pivotal to the spirit of the family. The words of Jesus recorded in Matthew 12:25 warn, "Every kingdom divided against itself is brought to desolation; and every city or house divided against itself shall not stand."

The young woman's shoulders were slumped and her eyes were rimmed with tears. Her husband appeared tense and uneasy. They had come for counseling at the wife's insistence. She was frustrated with her children. It seemed that even though she tried to do the right "parenting things," her children were spinning farther and farther out of control. "I read the books, and I think that I am doing a fairly consistent job with them. I just don't understand why things don't get better."

"What about your husband?" Tim probed, "Are you two in agreement on training and discipline? Where does he stand in all of this?"

The mother rolled her eyes and sighed in frustration. "He doesn't agree with my ideas. His parents raised him differently. He thinks I'm all wrong."

The husband countered, "I'm doing my best to work hard and bring home a paycheck for my family. I get home exhausted at the end of the day, and she expects me to take over with the kids. She nags me about it until I just want to leave."

"No, he is lazy; he comes home and plops himself down on the couch. He really is completely useless as a father," the young woman blurted as she burst into tears.

We waited patiently until the couple's stories wound down. Then we steered the counseling session in a direction that surprised them both. We taught them the number one parenting principle: Couples must focus on creating a strong marriage relationship because strong families grow out of solid marriages. Some couples don't recognize the danger of focusing solely on their children to the neglect of their marriage. It may be done in innocent excitement and a desire to do well with their children. Or it may also be done as a convenient distraction away from an already fragile marriage. Either way, failure to build a strong marriage spells failure to build a strong family. Children need the security of knowing that Daddy and Mommy are committed to loving each other and to giving their marriage relationship top priority. Let's look at three vital components of a great marriage. These are time together, effective communication, and unity.

> Happy marriages begin when we marry the ones we love, and they blossom when we love the ones we marry.
> – Tom Mullen

Time

During the getting-to-know-you phase and courtship period, we spend countless hours together. We look for excuses to enjoy the precious companionship of our love. But after the wedding and honeymoon, as our distractions and obligations multiply, we must carve out time in our hectic schedules for one another and diligently guard these moments. It's too easy to hustle from one activity to another, to the neglect of what should be our highest priority. The irony is that the most genuinely important things are the least demanding and the easiest to ignore. Here are a few ways to foster that all-important time together.

Debrief daily

Train yourselves and your children that when Daddy comes home from work, he and Mommy get 15 minutes of uninterrupted conversation. As Daddy arrives at home, the children get to bestow their hugs and kisses and briefly tell their exciting news of the day. Then they can be excused to their own activities while Mommy and Daddy settle down on the couch for a few minutes of adult conversation. Better yet, before the children leave the room, teach them to help Daddy take off his shoes and to thank him for his hard work. Acknowledge his hard work with a cold glass of lemonade, settle into the living room couch, and catch up on the day. This is *not* the time for Mommy to unload her frustration about the mischief little Billy got into, or to complain that she doesn't get enough money for the grocery budget. Nor is it the time for Daddy to notice the unfolded laundry that still sits on the loveseat. It is a time to reconnect after the separate business of the day. It is a time for the children to see that Daddy and Mommy love and value each other's company.

Note: The excitement for Daddy's homecoming is generated by Mama's excitement. The level of respect and thoughtfulness that parents show to one another as marriage partners will translate into the respect the children show their parents. We teach our children either on purpose or by default!

Make time for regular dates

Again, when we were first in love, even the simplest reason to be together was a celebration. We didn't need to go to the Fairmont to feel the excitement of a special evening together. However, our "dates" as a married couple required more creativity than money. In our penny-poor situation, we traded babysitting with other couples. Occasionally, we would take the children to a friend's for the evening and come home to a candlelight dinner for two. Or we ate dinner as a family and went out for an ice cream as a couple. We tried, even in our younger and financially leaner years, to get away together for a weekend every few months. Time without the little ones' constant neediness was rejuvenating and romantic.

> The cure for love is marriage, and the cure for marriage is love again.
>
> – Unkown

Summits

When we married in the early 1980s, our then President Ronald Reagan and Soviet Leader Mikhail Gorbachev were negotiating the end of the Cold War. They would meet periodically at superpower summits to discuss their political differences and to negotiate compromises for the good of world peace. We took note of these meetings and began having summits of our own; we were two distinctly different individuals attempting to meld our opinions and ideals into one workable and peaceable kingdom. Every month or two we would schedule a dinner date with the express purpose of discussing frustrations, parenting strategies, and areas of concern about each of our young children. It was understood that this date was not a prelude to "a little night music;" rather, it was a monthly staff meeting between president and vice president to insure the continuing health and development of our family.

Schedule a Summit Now!

Summits are so important that you should schedule one with your spouse right away while the idea is fresh.

Communication

Another building block of a strong marriage is good communication. What happens during daily debriefings, dates, and summits is the exchange of feelings, thoughts, ideas, and dreams. Libraries are full of books on the subject of improving communication, so we will not presume to address every facet of it. But we will offer a few points to ponder.

Avoid the "blame game"

The second sin recorded in the book of Genesis is blaming. Eve ate the fruit, then Adam ate the fruit. When God confronted them, Adam promptly blamed Eve, and Eve blamed the snake. Blaming is not taking ownership of our own shortcomings but manufacturing excuses for them.

"You are always too harsh with the children," she accuses.

"Well, if you weren't such a pushover with them, I wouldn't have to be the bad guy," he retaliates.

Blaming one another puts up walls of defense and anger that hinder resolution and unity. In counseling with married couples in conflict, we often ask them to consider what percentage of their problem belongs to each of them.

"I'm probably 20% to blame," one says.

The other retorts, "Ha! You are more like 80% at fault."

Or they martyr themselves, saying, "No, it's probably *all* my fault."

They finally give an honest evaluation. We then turn to Matthew chapter seven where Jesus admonishes us to consider the beam in our own eye rather than the mote in our brother's eye. In other words, Jesus teaches us to work on our own shortcomings. When we stop blaming our mate and work on our own weaknesses, the argument diffuses and healing begins. How much more harmony and growth there would be in our marriages if we concentrated on working out our "own salvation with fear and trembling" (Phil. 2:12).

Beware of using superlatives

"You always…" "I never…" "…Every time…" "All…" "…None…" Using superlatives is another form of the blame game and is a quick way to stir up strife. When you use "always" or "never," etc., it provokes your spouse and, ironically, discredits you. For example, when a husband accuses, "You never have dinner ready on time," can he really prove that, without exception, dinner has never once been on time? The wife immediately bristles into a defensive stance, shutting off further communication. She can probably recall the exact dates (few they may be) that dinner has been timely. Do you see the point? Good communication in marriage depends on the willingness of both spouses to stop putting up walls of defense. We'll override our own advice and use a superlative to make our point: *Never* say never.

> Marriages are made in heaven. But, again, so are thunder, lightning, tornadoes, and hail.
> – Unknown

Instead, use "I feel" or "I need"

An effective strategy to defuse the blame game is to begin a statement with "I feel" or "I need." When a wife says, "You never show me any respect in front of the kids," the husband will, most likely, become defensive—she has just blamed him for doing something wrong. Rephrasing the sentence using "I feel" removes the sting and changes the tone of the conversation: "*I feel* embarrassed when you correct me in front of the kids. *I need* you to build me up to them, so they will respect me and my authority." Using this phrasing requires the offended spouse to identify exactly what is bothersome and what she would like to see done. It also leaves no room for dispute. He cannot say, "Oh, no. You don't feel that way." A feeling is a feeling; it cannot be invalidated. Although this seems simplistic, it is a powerful way to discuss sensitive issues between mates. Try it!

Listen

Listening is the unsung hero of conversational skills. Rather than truly hearing what the other person is saying, we are often thinking about what our own next point will be. Fewer things are more frustrating than knowing that your beloved husband or wife is not hearing a word you are saying but is busy preparing his or her next salvo. Good listening is imperative to a healthy relationship. One way to ensure that you truly understand the essence of your spouse's conversation is the exercise of rephrasing. When she rephrases what she heard him say, he knows that she truly heard his thoughts correctly *or* that she misunderstood:

"So, you are saying that you would like dinner earlier than I have been making it lately?"

"Yes!"

"Okay, what time would you like it on the table?"

Then he can explain the thought further until they fully understand each other. Rephrasing is time consuming, but it is a great short-term exercise for couples that have constant misunderstandings. Confidence and trust are quickly rebuilt when you know that you are both being heard and understood.

Build your mate through encouragement

Admire and respect your spouse, and the same feelings will naturally trickle down to the children. The best example of this is the story, "Johnny Lingo's Eight Cow Wife":

"When I sailed to Kiniwata, an island in the Pacific, I took along a notebook. After I got back it was filled with descriptions of flora and fauna, native customs and costume. But the only note that still interests me is the one that says: 'Johnny Lingo gave eight cows to Sarita's father.' And I don't need to have it in writing. I'm reminded of it every time I see a woman belittling her husband or a wife withering under her husband's scorn. I want to say to them, 'You should know why Johnny Lingo paid eight cows for his wife.'"

Johnny Lingo wasn't exactly his name. But that's what Shenkin, the manager of the guesthouse on Kiniwata, called him. Shenkin was from Chicago and had a habit of Americanizing the names of the islanders. But Johnny was mentioned by many people in many connections. If I wanted to spend a few days on the neighboring island of Nurabandi, Johnny Lingo would put me up. If I wanted to fish he could show me where the biting was best. If it were pearls I sought, he would bring the best buys. The people of Kiniwata all spoke highly of Johnny Lingo, yet when they spoke they smiled, and the smiles were slightly mocking.

"Get Johnny Lingo to help you find what you want and let him do the bargaining," advised Shenkin. "Johnny knows how to make a deal."

"Johnny Lingo! A boy seated nearby hooted the name and rocked with laughter.

"What goes on?" I demanded. "Everybody tells me to get in touch with Johnny Lingo and then breaks up. Let me in on the joke."

"Oh, the people like to laugh," Shenkin said, shrugging. "Johnny's the brightest, the strongest young man in the islands. And for his age, the richest."

"But if he's all you say, what is there to laugh about?"

"Only one thing. Five months ago, at fall festival, Johnny came to Kiniwata and found himself a wife. He paid her father eight cows!

I knew enough about island customs to be impressed. Two or three cows would buy a fair-to-middling wife, four or five a highly satisfactory one. "Good Lord!" I said, "Eight cows! She must have beauty that takes your breath away." "She's not ugly," he conceded, and smiled a little. "But the kindest could only call Sarita plain. Sam Karoo, her father, was afraid she'd be left on his hands."

"But then he got eight cows for her? Isn't that extraordinary?"

"Never been paid before."

"Yet you call Johnny's wife plain?"

"I said it would be kindness to call her plain. She was skinny. She walked with her shoulders hunched and her head ducked. She was scared of her own shadow."

"Well," I said, "I guess there's just no accounting for love."

"True enough," agreed the man. "And that's why the villagers grin when they talk about Johnny. They get special satisfaction from the fact that the sharpest trader in the islands was bested by dull old Sam Karoo."

"But how?"

"No one knows and everyone wonders. All the cousins were urging Sam to ask for three cows and hold out for two until he was sure Johnny would pay only one. Then Johnny came to Sam Karoo and said, 'Father of Sarita, I offer eight cows for your daughter.'"

"Eight cows," I murmured. "I'd like to meet this Johnny Lingo."

"And I wanted fish. I wanted pearls. So the next afternoon I beached my boat at Nurabandi. And I noticed as I asked directions to Johnny's house that his name brought no sly smile to the lips of his fellow Nurabandians. And when I met the slim, serious young man, when he welcomed me with grace to his home, I was glad that from his own people he had respect unmingled with mockery. We sat in his house and talked. Then he asked, "You come here from Kiniwata?"

"Yes."

"They speak of me on that island?"

"They say there's nothing I might want they you can't help me get."

He smiled gently. "My wife is from Kiniwata."

"Yes, I know."

"They speak of her?"

"A little."

"What do they say?"

"Why, just..." The question caught me off balance. "They told me you were married at festival time."

"Nothing more?" The curve of his eyebrows told me he knew there had to be more.

They also say the marriage settlement was eight cows." I paused.

"They wonder why."

"They ask that?" His eyes lightened with pleasure. "Everyone in Kiniwata knows about the eight cows?"

I nodded.

"And in Nurabandi everyone knows it too." His chest expanded with satisfaction. "Always and forever, when they speak of marriage settlements, it will be remembered that Johnny Lingo paid eight cows for Sarita."

So that's the answer, I thought: vanity.

And then I saw her. I watched her enter the room to place flowers on the table. She stood still a moment to smile at the young man beside me. Then she went swiftly out again. She was the most beautiful woman I have ever seen. The lift of her shoulders, the tilt of her chin the sparkle of her eyes all spelled a pride to which no one could deny her the right. I turned back to Johnny Lingo and found him looking at me. "You admire her?" he murmured. "She...she's glorious. But she's not Sarita from Kiniwata," I said.

"There's only one Sarita. Perhaps she does not look the way they say she looked in Kiniwata." "She doesn't. I heard she was homely. They all make fun of you because you let yourself be cheated by Sam Karoo."

"You think eight cows were too many?" A smile slid over his lips. "No. But how can she be so different?"

"Do you ever think," he asked, "what it must mean to a woman to know that her husband has settled on the lowest price for which she can be bought? And then later, when the women talk, they boast of what their husbands paid for them. One says four cows, another maybe six. How does she feel, the woman who was sold for one or two?" This could not happen to my Sarita."

"Then you did this just to make your wife happy?"

"I wanted Sarita to be happy, yes. But I wanted more than that. You say she is different; this is true. Many things can change a woman. Things that happen inside, things that happen outside. But the thing that matters most is what she thinks about herself. In Kiniwata, Sarita believed she was worth nothing. Now she knows she is worth more than any other woman in the islands."

"Then you wanted -"

"I wanted to marry Sarita. I loved her and no other woman."

"But —" I was close to understanding.

"But," he finished softly, "I wanted an eight-cow wife."[5]

Unity

Of the many facets of marriage that directly affect children, either positively or negatively, few are as vital as our last area of discussion: unity and agreement. As we stated in the opening paragraph of this chapter, a house divided against itself shall not stand. Even the smallest child can sense when Mommy and Daddy are not getting along or have just had a disagreement. When two different sets of standards exist in a home, the children become confused and insecure. And even though they are immature, some children are wily enough to take advantage of the double standard and pit one parent against the other to satisfy their own desires. Again, this is not an exhaustive list but here are three important skills for strengthening unity in marriage:

Praise in public, correct in private

When you are in public, do not correct or criticize your spouse or reveal sensitive, intimate details, even in jest. We hadn't been married long when Tim came across a quote by then IBM president, Buck Rogers. Rogers had attributed his success as leader of the international company, in part, to his motto, "Praise in public, criticize in private." At that time we had fallen into the destructive habit of publicly finding fault with one another. It was embarrassing and maddening to have our private struggles aired, even in a small group of good friends. We decided to adopt the motto as our own, except that we replaced the negative word, *criticize*, with a more positive word, *correct*. (Criticism, no matter how well meant, is unproductive). As simple as this sounds, if one of us slipped up, the other had only to say the word, *praise,* and the criticizer knew it was time to change the course of the conversation. This little reminder kept us respectful and united. Over time, small changes can add up to bountiful blessings in a family.

> ## Praise in public, criticize in private.
> – Buck Rogers

Agree on parenting standards and family rules

Rarely do two people have exactly the same desires and expectations from parenting. Because methods and means are as diverse as spouses are individualistic, conflict is inevitable. Summits can be used to discuss, revise, and adjust the family rules so that both parents are united in their desires and expectations. We used summits to formulate and write out our family standards so that everyone was clear on what was expected. (Don't skip ahead, but chapter six is about the value of written standards, and it includes our own family standards.)

The unity between spouses is pivotal to the spirit of the family.

Stand behind your spouse's judgments

It is natural to occasionally disagree with a spouse's decision; however, it is inappropriate and unacceptable to undermine a spouse's respectability or authority in the presence of the children. Even if Dad's tone and manner seem harsh, there is no gain in saying, "Honey, don't take it out on Joey." This only angers the husband and shows little Joey that Mom and Dad disagree. Joey soon loses reverence for Dad and learns to be a manipulator. It also places an ugly wedge between parents. Such disagreements should be discussed beyond the earshot of the children. This reinforces the importance of our little motto, "Praise in public, correct in private."

We will close this chapter with a poignant story about a couple whose names will be Jason and Lindsey. They, along with their three children, lived for the Lord. Jason was an usher and a pillar in his local church, and Lindsey was a help and a strength to the pastor's wife and family. Their children were integral and popular members of the youth group. They seemed to have a good marital relationship and were actively involved in many aspects of church life and activities. Then, seemingly without warning, Jason disappeared. He later resurfaced across the country with the young and beautiful wife of another man. Devastated, Lindsey was left to raise three young teenage children alone. She stayed in church, struggling to keep the family together. But, one by one, the children fell away from God and into lives of sin and sadness. The sons drifted in and out of the drug and crime cultures. The daughter had three children by three different men, two of whom she briefly married. Lindsey is now a grandmother, raising the children of one of her irresponsible sons.

How did this family fall apart? It may be simplistic to reduce it down to one error, but the marriage had a primary flaw. Although Jason and Lindsey loved each other, they made the mistake of becoming increasingly child focused. During the harried years when the children were toddlers and preteens, they stopped nurturing their marriage relationship. Just as a plant that is denied water and sunlight will eventually die, a marriage that is bereft of nurture and attention will eventually wither.

Remember, it's SIMPLE...

- The optimal effectiveness of your parenting and the success of your children are directly tied to the strength of love and commitment in your marriage. The unity between spouses is pivotal to the spirit of the family.

- There is a danger among couples to focus solely on their children once they arrive, to the neglect of their marriage.

- Children need the security of knowing that daddy and mommy are committed and love each other and regard their marriage with primary importance.

- We must carve out **time** in our hectic schedules for one another:

    Debrief Daily - It is a time to reconnect after the separate business of the day.

Make time for regular dates - Time without the little one's constant neediness is rejuvenating and romantic.

Have routine Summits - Schedule a dinner date every month or two with the expressed purpose of discussing frustrations, parenting strategies, and areas of concern with each of your young children.

- Practice these important **communication** tools:

  Avoid the 'Blame Game' - Blaming one another puts up walls of defense and anger that hinders resolution and unity.

  Beware of using superlatives - **NEVER say Never.**

  Use 'I Feel,' 'I Need'- **Using this phrasing requires the offended spouse to identify exactly what it is that is bothersome, and what they would like to see done.**

- **Listening** is the unsung hero of conversation skills:

  Build Your Mate through Encouragement - Be an example of admiration and respect to your spouse.

- Foster the three important skills for strengthening **unity** in marriage:

  Praise in public, correct in private - Never correct or criticize your spouse or reveal sensitive intimate details, even in jest, in public.

  Agree on parenting standards and family rules- It is during your summits that you can discuss and sometimes revise and adjust your family rules so that both parents are united in their desires and expectations.

  Stand behind your spouse's judgments - **It**

is natural to occasionally disagree with a decision made by your spouse; however, it is unacceptable to undermine their respectability or authority, regarding correction, in the presence of the children.

- Remember - Since time together fostering our marriage is too important not to schedule, put a date on the calendar while this is fresh in your reading. Do it now! We mean it!

PART ONE

HELPING YOUR CHILD
Become...

SELF-CONTROLLED

Chapter Three
THE HUMAN
CONDITION

*D*uring the past few generations, humanistic philosophies that insist on the inherent goodness of the child have seeped into our society. We are increasingly bombarded with humanistic arguments that all children are innately good and naturally seek to do right. "How could such a chubby-cheeked angel be marred by sin?" they ask. Humanists advocate negotiation and reasoning with the immature minds of two- and three-year-olds. They vehemently argue against the biblical use of the rod and reproof in training our children, calling it hitting and abuse. Their relentless diatribes have confused many well-meaning Christian parents who now feel guilty and fearful when they use scriptural child training methods. Before we proceed with the how and why of biblical child training, we find it necessary to address humankind's sinful nature and tendency to rebel and to learn to recognize rebellion in our children and ourselves. The human will must be brought under subjection, and self-control established as the foundation of Christian maturity. All growth and success in life depends on first establishing self-control.

Guilty Stain

Disregarding God's authority, Adam and Eve chose to eat the fruit of the tree. Their disobedience brought the stain of sin that mars all of humanity. We wrestle with self-indulgent sin and guilt daily. We are surrounded by people satisfying their cravings with over-eating, reckless spending, indulging in sexual immorality, greed, dishonest business practices, and other selfish acts. Temperance and self-restraint appear to be misconstrued as prudish values of the past. But God's Word repeatedly warns us of the danger in allowing the carnal nature to run unchecked and instructs us to restrain our flesh. "For to be *carnally minded* is *death*; but to be *spiritually minded* is *life and peace*. Because the carnal mind is enmity against God: for it is not subject to the law of God, neither indeed can be" (Romans 8: 6,7). "*So then they that are in the flesh cannot please God*" (Romans 8:8). Yes, that chubby-cheeked cherub is selfish in his desires and needs. The tendency to be carnally minded is not developed as a child grows, but it is an inborn trait that must be recognized and bent by wise, loving parents from the beginning of life.

When a child is very young and his reasoning abilities are still immature and undeveloped, God does not count his actions as sin. "Therefore to him that knoweth to do good, and doeth it not, to *him* it is sin" (James 4:17). Before the child can differentiate between right and wrong, or good and evil, he is not sinning. Deuteronomy 1:39 makes the same point: "…and your children which in that day had no knowledge between good and evil…" Hebrews 5:13-14 concurs: "For everyone that useth milk is unskillful in the word of righteousness: for he is a babe.

But strong meat belongeth to them that are of full age, even those who by reason of use have their senses exercised to discern both good and evil." Although the young child is not blameworthy now, the day will soon come that he will comprehend good and evil and will be accountable for his understanding. As parents, we are commissioned by God to train up our children in the way they should go, teaching them knowledge of both good and evil, leading them to walk in the ways of righteousness. We are commanded to give them a taste for what is right. We are directed to be their conscience, recognizing sin and rebellion until the day of their understanding.

> Our earth is degenerate in these latter days; bribery and corruption are common; children no longer obey their parents; and the end of the world is evidently approaching.
>
> – Assyrian clay tablet 2800 B.C.

More than Obedience

We know that children, like their parents, wrestle with self-indulgence and self-willed behavior daily. When children buck against their parents' efforts to direct their behavior, it is clearly rebellion. It is vital that we learn to identify the face of rebellion. Webster defines rebellion as "an open and avowed renunciation of the authority of the government to which one owes allegiance or open resistance to lawful authority." God contrasts rebellion and blessing and their consequences in Isaiah 1:19-20: "If ye be willing and obedient, ye shall eat the good of the land: But if ye refuse and rebel, ye shall be devoured with the sword; for the mouth of the Lord hath spoken it." In order to be blessed with the good of the land it is not enough to simply perform the acts commanded of us. God insists that we do them willingly: develop a good attitude, obey readily and promptly, and act without reluctance or coercion. If our "obedience" is characterized by foot-stomping, defiant attitudes, we have indeed rebelled just as if we had thrust out our chest and shouted a blatant and defiant, "*No!*" to the face of God. Either way the sin is the same and the punishment decisive. I Samuel 15:22-23 displays God's outrage and intolerance for rebellion, saying, "Behold, to obey is better than sacrifice, and to hearken than the fat of rams. For rebellion is as the sin of witchcraft, and stubbornness is as iniquity and idolatry." Rebellion is fatal. It must be recognized and addressed.

Active Rebellion

Active rebellion is characterized by overt, blatant acts of disobedience, defiance, and disrespect to parental authority. Remember Webster defines it as "open resistance to lawful authority." It is certainly the more obvious sort of defiance to parental authority. Isaiah construes rebellion as being unwilling and disobedient. Consider these as examples of active rebellion[6]:

- Willfully and knowingly refusing to obey parental commands or established rules.

- A defiant "no," or any other verbal dissent or disrespect.

- Temper tantrums.

- Pouting, screaming, stiffening up.

- Resisting parent-led actions, i.e., jerking hand away, going limp when parent attempts to pick the child up

- Venting anger on objects: kicking or throwing things.

- Angry words, "I hate you, Mommy." "You're mean."

"What a jerk."

- Hitting parent.

Passive Rebellion

Although it is less obvious, passive rebellion is just as dangerous. Parents can easily overlook or allow passive rebellion because of its subtle nature. Remember that the two key ingredients of blessing are obedience and willingness. Willingness, again, implies obeying without complaint or delay. When we overlook protests, grumbling, and less obvious displays of challenge to our authority, we unwittingly strengthen the child's self-will and solidify his resolve to win. Here are some examples of passive rebellion[7]:

- Delayed obedience—"I'll be there in a minute." "After I finish this puzzle."

- Child bargains or negotiates—"I will, if..." "Can I do it later?"

- Ignoring instructions.

- Conditional obedience—"Why?" "Joey has to do it, too."

- Obeying with a bad attitude—stomping away, sighing, grumbling, crying while complying.

- Doing the job halfway, or not to the acceptable standard of quality.

- Complying, but doing it slowly.

The Protest

We learned the lesson of recognizing passive rebellion in a vivid way. When one of our sons was just over a year old, he began stiffening his legs and sticking out his little bottom when he did not get what he wanted. He accompanied his babyish protest with an award-winning, big-lipped, pouty face. It was just so cute! We giggled when he demonstrated his indignation, and even encouraged him to perform for our friends. In our ignorance we did not realize that we were also strengthening his self-will and teaching him to disobey his parents. Our amusement became dismay when the stiff-legged pout evolved into a full-fledged, floor-kicking tantrum. We finally realized our mistake. It took many concerted hours of correction to eradicate what we had not at first recognized as rebellion. Rebellion is not cute!

Self-Control

The Word of God strongly admonishes us to control our fleshly, carnal desires. The hallmark of Christian character is self-control. As we established earlier, we define self-control as not being ruled by passions, emotions, appetites, desires, wishes, or curiosity. Self-control is the deliberate choice to do right even when doing wrong looks like more fun. It is the freedom from having to do what one feels like doing. Self-control is being strong enough to say "no" to all selfish desires and to say "yes" to what is right. Very young children are not equipped to recognize selfish carnality or to be cleansed from guilt. We are called to introduce them to self-restraint, to bring judgment and consequence to their self-indulgent lives, and to bend them toward the right path. As this parental control is consistently exercised and explained, it slowly gives way to self-control. As the child matures,

Parent control → Self Control → God Control

he begins to understand the nature of good and evil. It is our responsibility to be our children's conscience while they are too immature to know better. Throughout this process, we are introducing the need for salvation by cleansing guilt and restoring relationship, which leads them to their ultimate goal, willful obedience to God. Steps to this foundational process will be addressed in the next chapter.

Caution

Dad, Mom, we cannot teach our children what we do not possess ourselves. Our example and not our words will be our children's greatest teacher. We cannot be willful and defiant and be blessed of God. We cannot grumble and resentfully follow God's ways and be blessed. Our habits and rebellious attitudes will be caught by our children regardless of how much we talk about obedience and submission to authority. Feeling convicted yet? As we strive to be better parents, we will really be striving to be better Christians ourselves. Our character and integrity must grow in order to instill the same character and integrity in our children. This is the very foundation of successful Christian living and the first goal of Christian parenting.

> Parents can TELL but never TEACH unless they PRACTICE what they PREACH.
> – Arnold Glasow

God's Chosen Daddy

When God sought to call a very special people for his name, He searched for a righteous man to lead his people. He chose Abraham. Why did He trust Abraham with this vast, far-reaching covenant responsibility? Genesis 18:19 explains, "For I know him, that he will command his children and his household after him, and they shall keep the way of the Lord, to do justice and judgment; that the Lord may bring upon Abraham that which he hath spoken of him." God knew that Abraham would not conform to the common parenting technique of simply providing food, clothing, shelter, and safety from harm. God was certain that Abraham would transcend the norm and lead his family in the way of righteousness. God bestowed the great blessing and responsibility of becoming the father of a nation as numerous as the sands of the sea on a man who would actively train his children in the ways of the Lord. Because of Abraham's diligence in godly leadership, God promised him that he would be the father of many nations and that his lineage would impact the world. God has kept His word.

Jewish people now reside on every continent of the world. Although they comprise only about 2% of America's population, Jewish people "are disproportionately influential in so many areas of American life. They are spoken of, written about, depicted far more than other groups of similar size."[8] They are a prosperous and blessed people, and their blessing began with one man who was a godly leader of his household. Christians, as the "branch grafted in" to the family of Abraham through adoption, are also blessed when we follow Abraham's example and command our children and households, and "keep the way of the Lord."

Remember, it's SIMPLE...

- Humanistic philosophies that insist on the inherent goodness of the child have seeped into our society.

- Their relentless diatribes have confused many well-meaning Christian parents who now feel guilty and fearful when they use scriptural child training methods.

- The hallmark of Christian character is self-control.

- The human will must be brought under subjection and self-control established as the foundation of Christian maturity. All growth and success in life depends on first establishing self-control.

- We must learn to recognize rebellion in our children and ourselves.

- Webster defines rebellion as "an open and avowed renunciation of the authority of the government to which one owes allegiance or open resistance to lawful authority."

- Active rebellion is characterized by overt, blatant acts of disobedience, defiance, and disrespect to parental authority.

- Although it is less obvious, passive rebellion is just as dangerous. Parents can easily overlook or allow passive rebellion because of its subtle nature.

- As parents, we are commissioned by God to train up our children in the way they should go. We are commanded to give them a taste for what is right. We are directed to be their conscience, recognizing sin and rebellion until the day of their understanding.

- God was certain that Abraham would transcend the norm and lead his family in the way of righteousness. God bestowed the great blessing and responsibility of becoming the father of a nation as numerous as the sands of the sea on a man who would actively train his children in the ways of the Lord. Because of Abraham's diligence in godly leadership, God promised him that he would be the father of many nations and that his lineage would impact the world. God has kept His word.

Chapter Four
BEARING PEACEABLE FRUIT

*T*he harried young mother sits at the kitchen table. She does not care that her forearm is stuck in a half-dried pool of apple juice. It is naptime, the blessed hour of peace in her otherwise chaotic home. She surveys the wreckage that was only this morning an orderly family room. Toys are flung helter-skelter. Cereal crumbs are crushed into the recently vacuumed carpet. A banana peel is drooping on the arm of the sofa. She is teetering on the verge of despair.

She sighs when she recalls the pitying glances and whispered conversation she overheard last Sunday night after she had wrestled with her four year old son all through service. "What that little one needs is a firm spanking. He runs his mother ragged. It's a shame; he is headed for trouble…"

"A good spanking?" she thinks, "I can't spank my baby. I love him too much to hit him."

And then the Holy Ghost speaks to the young mother's weary heart: "He who spares his rod hates his son: but he that loves him chastens him often. Do not be deceived, daughter. You do not love your son if you do not discipline him early and diligently (Hebrews 12:11). Chasten your son while there is hope, and let not your soul spare for his crying (Proverbs 19:18). There is still great hope for him, for he is young. Hope will fade later on if you neglect correction."

> Chasten your son while there is hope, and let not your soul spare for his crying.
>
> – Proverbs 19:18

"He is young; his tantrums and disobediences are only childishness," the young mother excuses her son's naughtiness.

"Foolishness is bound up in the heart of a child, but the rod of correction will drive it far from him (Proverbs 22:15)," comes the patient reply of the Holy Ghost.

"Would you have me be cruel and *hit* my son?" asks the doubtful mother.

"Withhold not correction from the child for if you spank him with the rod, he shall not die. Thou shall strike him with the rod, and deliver his soul from hell (Proverbs 23:13-14). You are cruel if you do not chastise him in love, which is necessary to keep him from perishing." How patiently the Lord speaks to our human folly.

"If I spank him, I will stifle his creativity. I want him to feel free to express himself," she finds herself objecting.

"On the contrary, my daughter," comes the Holy Ghost's response. "The rod and reproof give wisdom" (Proverbs 29:15).

"But won't he turn from me when he is older?" She worries.

But the Holy Ghost says, "Correct your son, and he will give you rest; he will bring delight to your soul (Proverbs 29:17). It is correcting him early, and bending him in the way that he should go that will bring delight to your soul. This is your promise, Dear One. But be warned, a child left to himself brings his mother to shame" (Proverbs 29:15).[9]

Time out!

As our society spirals rapidly downward and its philosophies stray farther and farther from the timeless truths of God's Word, we are increasingly bombarded with humanistic arguments against the use of the rod and reproof in training our children. But as our young mother was mercifully reminded, the eternally valid, living Word of God repeatedly instructs, admonishes, and warns us about the life-saving value

> **Time out will not train our children.**

of physical chastisement. Time out will not train our children. Cooing, cajoling and attempting bribery through reasoning and logic will not bring self-control to a willful child. Grounding, restricting, and denying privileges are not effective means of leading our children in the way of righteousness. It is both foolish pride and a lie from hell to believe that we can save the souls of our children without correctly administering biblical chastisement and instruction. And we as parents sin when we know to do right and do it not (James 4:17) because it is not comfortable to us! The key is *correctly* administering the rod and reproof. It must always be administered calmly and lovingly with the objective of training the child in the way that he should go—not as punishment or in an "I'll show *you* who's boss" frustrated attitude.

As the Lord corrected the confused mother above, we must resist the popular belief, held even among some Christians, that children are inherently good. The idea that if children are given positive direction and reinforcement for right behavior they will grow wise and responsible is unbiblical! As the Holy Ghost told our young mother, all children are sinful and foolish and need chastisement (spankings) to align their hearts with God. When Susie throws a tantrum, we tend to excuse her sinful behavior: she is tired, hungry, shy, or just not feeling social. The Word of God tells us the opposite: "The heart is deceitful above all things, and desperately wicked: who can know it?" (Jeremiah 17:9). We must deal with rebellion, whether active or passive, the biblical way: with the rod and reproof.

HOW?

Proper and productive chastisement is not complex; it consists of five basic steps done calmly and clearly in a private place. When the child has rebelled either actively or passively:

1.

Take the child *calmly* to the "place of cleansing."

The first element of proper correction has little to do with Junior's infraction but everything to do with your attitude and self-control as the parent. Do not wait until you are at the end of your patience or cannot maintain peaceful resolve and demeanor. Don't humiliate your child (and in the process, yourself) in front of others. Do not yell at Junior, but coolly take him by the hand and lead him to a quiet, private place. Publicly denigrating or berating a child will never encourage him to make a positive change, just as the boss at work would only humiliate and anger you if he took you to task in front of co-workers or customers. The Bible tells parents not to provoke to anger or enrage their children (Colossians 3:21,

Ephesians 6:4). Losing control discredits our teaching, for how can we teach the child self-control if we have just shown by our blowup that we do not ourselves possess it? Children can spot hypocrisy in a minute. Humiliation only serves to break the bonds of loving relationship; it is never productive. We must maintain the dignity of the child and conduct ourselves with decorum and respectability at all times.

2.

Be sure the child understands what the infraction is.

Recount the offense. We refer to our family's written standards (we discuss them at length in chapter six) when there is a rebellious act or attitude that needs to be corrected. To be sure that the child understands his wrong, we ask him to tell us what he did to earn the correction. Recounting the offense is also a form of confessing his sin. Good spiritual training includes teaching him to be accountable for wrongdoing. If we spank before we are sure that the child clearly understands what he did, we are not correcting a wrong action or attitude, but frustrating and angering our child. However, this is not the time to engage in lengthy lecture. The child is anticipating the coming chastisement at this point and is less receptive to your reproof. First cleanse with the rod and then instruct and reprove briefly while the clay of the child's heart is pliable and easily molded.

> To be sure that the child understands his wrong, we ask him to tell us what he did to earn the correcting.

3.

Chastise.

Using a small neutral object, swat the child on the bottom. The hand is an instrument of love and nurture and should not be used in chastisement. Scripture clearly teaches the use of the "rod" in correction, not the hand. And where should we spank? The Book of Proverbs provides plain instructions: "...the rod is for the fool's back" (10:13), "...and stripes for the back of fools" (19:29), "...a rod for the fool's back" (26:3). The Hebrew word for *back* in each of these Scriptures is the word, *gev*, meaning "middle back of the body, the part of the anatomy that is of soft composition and lacks vital organs." Simply put, spank the bottom. Hitting a child in anger for the purpose of hurting him shows your anger and lack of self-control. Walk away until you can chastise calmly and productively. While swatting, talk slowly and deliberately to the child about his transgression until he displays remorse and compliance. Require the child to bend over your lap or over the bed, be as still as is reasonable for his or her age and level of maturity, and receive the correction with quiet whimpering. Protesting, screaming, wiggling away, and deflecting swats with his hands are all signs of rebellion, and they should add to the chastisement. Be discerning of your child's countenance and spirit when you have finished the actual chastisement. Expect tears of sorrow, but you should not sense anger or feel any resistance to you personally. If you do, this is evidence that the chastisement is incomplete and you must go through the process again to correct the attitude. The purpose of the rod is to bring the child to repentance; you are only finished with this step when he is contrite and humble.

4.

Reprove.

The child's will is made receptive and open through chastisement and is ready for instruction in righteousness. Now is the time to instruct and encourage. Reproof is literally re-proving, reasoning, and teaching with words. Your attitude during this time should be clear of any frustration or anger that the offense provoked; the child has received his physical reward for his misdeed and is ready to repent and ask for God's power to overcome the temptation in the future. Show him that a loving parent, modeling the perfect love of his Heavenly Father, is quick to forgive. It can truly be a very spiritual time. The carefully chosen, lovingly spoken, biblically-based words you speak at this time "sink in" like nothing else will. "For the word of God is quick and powerful, and sharper than any two-edged sword, piercing even to the dividing asunder of soul and spirit, and of the joints and marrow, and is a discerner of the thoughts and intents of the heart" (Hebrews 4:12). Do not underestimate the impact of this moment; rushing past this step is missing a critical opportunity to effect positive change.

5.

Restore relationship.

This step is so closely connected with the previous one that it is hard to separate, but we will isolate it here in order to discuss it and bring this vital component of the correction process into sharper focus. Because disobedience and rebellion is clearly sin against God as well as man, lead your child in a prayer of

You are modeling the beauty of the love and forgiveness Jesus has extended to us.

repentance for the specific act and restoration after your reproof. Ask Jesus to forgive him for the specific sin, thank Him for forgiveness, and ask Him to give strength and help to do right the next time. What an opportunity to teach him to fall at the feet of Jesus for forgiveness, receive cleansing, and ask for help to do things right!

Nothing opens a child's spirit like lovingly administered correction by rod and reproof. Be sure to capitalize on the tenderness that using the rod creates to build relationship with your child. Oftentimes the little one will want to climb on Daddy's lap after a "cleansing" session. When the rod and reproof have been administered properly and the child has been forgiven and restored, he will want to restore relationship with you. Never shun the child or show any residual frustration. By showing him forgiveness and the unconditional love of Jesus, you are cementing the understanding within his mind that God is truly forgiving and loving. You are modeling the beauty of the love and forgiveness Jesus has extended to us. Always leave hugging and smiling.

Heart of Anger

Parental attitude throughout this process is so crucial that it merits repeated emphasis. Don't take your child's disobedience as a personal affront. Foolishness is bound in the heart of every child, and his sinful actions should not surprise you or be taken as a personal insult. Don't let emotions or pride get in the way of proper correction. Understanding the true nature and tendencies of your child will help you deal with his actions in a matter-of-fact manner and without doubt or guilt. Correction done from a heart of anger or in frustration is not only ineffective; it is counter-productive. Incorrect discipline is as detrimental as no discipline.

"Come to Mommy, Sweetheart."

The little sweetheart laughingly runs the other way.

"Did you hear me? I said come here." With a catch-me-if-you-can expression tossed over her shoulder, the race is on. Mommy darts this way, while Sweetheart runs that way, "You had better stop this minute. I said stop."

Sweetheart knows from much experience that Mommy isn't quite at the end of her emotional rope yet. She can tell by the pitch of Mama's voice and the color of her face that she doesn't mean business quite yet. After all, it's fun to play this game with Mama, and Sweetheart knows just how far she can stretch the rope. "I'm going to count to three, and you had better come to me if you know what's good for you."

Uh-oh, thinks the little darling, the party is almost over. She's going to start counting. But I still have a few last seconds of fun.

"One...two...two and a haaaaalf...okay, that's it. I'm not playing anymore. You're gonna get it!" Mama does her best to reach and grab. With one final swoop, the little sweetheart is caught. Mama's hair is disheveled, her face is red, and her blood pressure is elevated. She is annoyed, personally insulted, and now angry. She now intends to make her child "pay" for the scene.

Making a child "pay" for her actions is simply punishment. When an angry parent uses physical punishment against a child who has disobeyed and brought frustration, she is simply bullying someone smaller than her into submission. The motivation behind punishment is generally anger and retribution; it shows immaturity and lack of self-control. True love does what is best, not what feels best at the time.

Calmly and Clearly ONE Time

Rules and expectations should be consistent and reasonable; we must first establish reasonable standards of behavior that everyone clearly understands. Consistency is the key to parenting success. We must teach our children that we mean what we say. Anything less than 100% consistency on our part sets us all up for frustration.

Like our example of little sweetheart and her mother, parents and children often fall into a frustrating and counterproductive game. Father or mother gives a command that he or she would like the child to obey but doesn't really expect him to right away. The child hears the command, doesn't feel like obeying, and knows from experience that she can ignore it for at least a few minutes, or until the parental tone of voice hits that fevered pitch. The cycle of command, ignore, frustrate, command and threaten, disregard, bluster, and finally parental anger and child's fear reinforces two negative situations. For the parent, being seemingly disregarded as the child's ultimate influence and authority leads to guilt, despair, and the feeling of failure. For the child, it strengthens her belief that it is not necessary to listen to or obey her parent the first time. It nullifies the parent's word and mocks his or her authority. When the little sweetheart thinks that she can get away with ignoring Mama one time, she is willing to try it 99 times to find the one! A directive given calmly and clearly one time should be all the direction given. The consequence for not obeying the *first* command should be given calmly and swiftly. We must be 100% consistent and reasonable in our expectations. We will expand on this idea in the next two chapters.

> Tend your garden every day, lest your young ones go astray.
> – Unknown

Betimes

At first, chastisement will be administered often. Do not be discouraged. "I spank and spank, but it seems to do no good," many parents say, but when questioned, they find that they have been making some basic parenting mistakes. When a standard of behavior is established such as, "We will speak to you calmly and clearly *one* time," we are all bound to follow it. As we just stated above, if we speak two, three, four times, we are not following our own standard. If we find ourselves frustrated, it is most often because we have issued a directive, have not been obeyed the first time, and have not administered correction for it. If we are inconsistent, our little cherubs will certainly try us. They have little to lose and everything to gamble if they know that we are more bluster than bite. If we want to be listened to and obeyed on the first command, we must commit to follow through with immediate consequences. As often as we are disobeyed, we *must* follow through with consequences. You will find that as you become consistent and diligent, you will spend less time using the rod.

Instrument of Obedience

The Bible does not, to our knowledge, instruct parents to strike their children with their hands. The hands are instruments of loving affection. The Word repeatedly instructs parents to use a "rod" in chastisement. The Hebrew word for rod is *shebet*, which means "reed, shoot, or switch." A broad flat wooden paddle similar to a five-gallon paint stir or some type of textile or

> **The rod and reproof give wisdom.**
> – Proverbs 29:15

leather material about as big as a good-sized bookmarker is appropriate.

Warning: The purpose of the rod is not to inflict wounds or bruise the child, but to be a stinging consequence to sin and a reminder to bring the child back under parental authority.

The rod and reproof give wisdom (Proverbs 29:15).

The Secret Ingredient

We must also be sure that our chastisement is accompanied by instruction. Remember, the rod *and reproof* give wisdom (Proverbs 29:15). It is important to speak to the child as he is being chastised. Simply state, "When Daddy says stop (swat), that means stop (swat). I expect you to say 'Yes, Sir,' and stop right then (swat). Do you understand, Son? (swat)."

When your child has received loving, consistent, chastisement, he will not fight but submit willingly to your correction. It is important to be alert to his heart condition and attitude toward you.

Attitude IS Everything

A rebellious act is the fruit of a rebellious attitude. We must be keenly sensitive to bad attitudes before they become rebellious acts. By the time it is an action, such as a door slammed in anger at a parental directive, the attitude is firmly established and will take blood, sweat, and tears to eradicate. Review the signs of passive rebellion listed in the previous chapter for the roots of bad attitudes.

> A rebellious act is the fruit of a rebellious attitude.

We must remember that the two elements of blessing are willingness (attitude) and obedience (action).

At the risk of being redundant we will say again that the one and only purpose of chastisement is to bring repentance and restore right relationship with parent and God. The correction is complete only when the child's attitude is sweet and remorseful. Your child will naturally reach up to you for a hug and the relationship will be restored. If the child still displays a defiant or angry attitude, a transformation of the heart has obviously not taken place. The process should be repeated. Yes, repeated.

Be Encouraged!

Dad and Mom, do you desire peace and blessing in your home? Do you want to enjoy your children and be honored by them for years to come? The Bible has a promise and an admonition that we should all commit to memory and post throughout our homes: "Now no chastisement for the present seemeth to be joyous, but grievous: nevertheless afterward it yieldeth the peaceable fruit of righteousness unto them which are exercised thereby" (Hebrews 12:11). Remember chastisement does seem dreadful at times, for parent as well as child. The need for correction seems to come at some of the most inconvenient, embarrassing, and aggravating times; however, obeying what God has explicitly directed in His Word will never be a waste of time or energy. Do not despair when your children seem to have bottoms of stone, or when it seems that they just aren't getting it. There is no child, no not one, that will not eventually succumb to God's divine design for child training. God's Word cannot lie; it *will* yield a peaceful and beautiful relationship between you and your children. Be not weary in well doing, and endure hardship like a good soldier! In doing so, you will experience a miracle. The Bible calls it "the peaceable fruit of righteousness."

Remember, it's SIMPLE...

• The eternally valid, living Word of God repeatedly instructs, admonishes, and warns us about the life-saving value of physical chastisement:

> "He who spares his rod hates his son: but he that loves him chastens him often" (Proverbs 13:24).

> "Foolishness is bound up in the heart of a child, but the rod of correction will drive it far from him" (Proverbs 22:15).

> "Withhold not correction from the child for if you spank him with the rod, he shall not die. Thou shall strike him with the rod, and deliver his soul from hell" (Proverbs 23:13-14).

> "The rod and reproof give wisdom" (Proverbs 29:15).

> "Correct your son, and he will give you rest; he will bring delight to your soul" (Proverbs 29:17).

> "A child left to himself brings his mother to shame" (Proverbs 29:15).

> "Now no chastisement for the present seemeth to be joyous, but grievous: nevertheless afterward it yieldeth the peaceable fruit of righteousness unto them which are exercised thereby" (Hebrews 12:11).

HOW?

1. Take them CALMLY to the "place of cleansing"— We must maintain the dignity of the child and conduct ourselves with decorum and respectability at all times.

2. Be sure the child understands what the infraction is. To be sure that the child understands his wrong, we ask him to tell us what he did to earn the correction.

3. Chastise—The purpose of the rod is to bring the child to repentance; you are only finished with this step when they are contrite and humble.

4.Reprove—Now is the time to instruct and encourage. Reproof is literally re-proving, reasoning, and teaching with words.

5. Restore relationship—Ask Jesus to forgive him for the specific sin, thank Him for forgiveness, and ask Him to give strength and help to do right the next time. By you showing him forgiveness and the unconditional love of Jesus, you are cementing that God is truly forgiving and loving. Always leave hugging and smiling.

• It is important to watch parental attitude. Don't take your child's disobedience as a personal affront. Don't let emotions or pride get in the way of proper correction.

• We must teach our children that we mean what we say. Anything less than 100% consistency on our part sets us all up for frustration.

• If we find ourselves frustrated, it is most often because we have issued a directive, have not been obeyed the first time, and have not corrected for it. We find that as we become consistent and diligent, we spend less time using the rod.

• A rebellious act is the fruit of a rebellious attitude. We must be keenly sensitive to bad attitudes before they become rebellious acts.

• God's word cannot lie; it will yield a peaceful and beautiful relationship between you and your children.

Be not weary in well doing, and you will experience a miracle.

Chapter Five
TRAIN UP A CHILD

*H*ave you ever considered God's decision to put the Tree of the Knowledge of Good and Evil in the midst of the garden? He left explicit "Do not touch" instructions. "And the Lord God commanded the man, saying, Of every tree of the garden thou mayest freely eat: But of the tree of the knowledge of good and evil, thou shall not eat of it: for in the day that thou eatest thereof thou shalt surely die" (Genesis 2: 16-17). God's command left no doubts. This tree was deadly; yet, curiously, He planted it in the middle of the garden.

The forbidden tree was beautiful and majestic. It was lofty and broad with glossy green foliage that shimmered as breezes rustled through its boughs. The sun glinted off the plump, fragrant fruit, hanging just within reach. The atmosphere that surrounded the tree was peaceful and inviting. This alluring tree stood in the center of Eden where it couldn't be ignored. Adam and Eve must have strolled around it and wondered at it on a daily basis. What a temptation! Though the other fruit trees were probably just as lovely, the very fact that it was forbidden made this tree all the more intriguing. Adam and Eve faced the same exercise in self-control that we face daily: follow the appetite of the flesh and do what we want, or overcome our fleshly desires, follow the Spirit, and do what we should.

The primary goal of Christian parenting is to teach our children self-control. We must train them to recognize evil, despise it, and choose to do right. This lesson is an incremental process. It requires daily exercises of self-control, layered day upon day, month upon month, and year upon year. "Precept upon precept, line upon line...here a little, and there a little"(Isaiah 28:10). It involves training their developing conscience. When they are very young, children do not have the cognitive ability to connect their actions with broad moral and eternal truths, so it is our responsibility to act as their conscience. Before their moral faculties are fully developed, we give them opportunities to deny their own wants and submit to authority. It begins with small lessons such as "Don't touch" and "Come to Mommy." Although these are not moral commands, they condition children to stop what they want to do (touch the pretty object or run from Mommy), and do promptly what their higher authority requires. It is easy for us to see these little conflicts as isolated incidents, disconnected from moral or spiritual training. On the contrary! In the midst of these little lessons is the shaping and strengthening of either the desire to follow fleshly lusts, or the will to deny carnal appetites and choose to do right. Remember that there is life and peace for those who follow biblical principles, but sin, guilt, and death for those who follow their carnal inclinations.

The Tree in the Midst of the Living Room

Like Adam and Eve's constant awareness of the shimmering tree in the midst of the garden, our children are confronted daily with temptations. It is to the profound benefit of our children that we provide opportunities inside our homes for self-control training, which will equip them for whatever enticements they face. To the toddler, Daddy's ring of keys is a glimmering attraction sitting on the coffee table. Mommy's purse, with those yummy mints and shiny pennies in it, is hanging on the back of her bedroom door. Fresh cookies are in the pantry. These enticing trinkets provide wonderful opportunities for proactive self-control training.

> Prepare the child for the path, not the path for the child.

When each of our children was able to toddle around and explore, between 15 and 18 months of age or earlier, we began presenting a "tree" of temptation within his or her reach for the purpose of training. The scenarios usually went something like this: Daddy laid his wallet and keys on an end table. He kept a watchful eye on the bait, knowing that her curiosity would draw her to it. "Don't touch, Honey," he said calmly, as her chubby little hand reached out to stroke the leather treasure. The hand retracted temporarily, but the session was then in full swing. She reached again for the object of her fascination. Daddy watched as she stole a glance at him, then picked up the wallet. He lowered himself to her eye level, and said quietly and firmly, "Put it down. Daddy said, 'Don't touch.'" He was setting up her understanding of the command, using the same words each time. When Daddy was certain she understood the words, and she touched the wallet again, he swatted her upper thigh smartly enough to sting and surprise, calmly saying, "Don't touch," again.

With some children, one time will cure the curiosity. The sting of correction outweighs the lure of the desired object, and conditioning for obedience is established. However, for some hardy youngsters, the exchange with Daddy only sweetens the temptation. This is not a personal insult; do not take it that way. Do not be offended or angered if your child tries you again…and again…and again. He or she is simply testing the strength of your resolve. When you engage in this training session, be willing to stay calm and persevere to victory. You must never, even in frustration or for lack of time, let the child win. This serves to teach them that Daddy or Mommy can be persuaded to give in to the child's whims and appetites if she wears you down and outlasts you. You will be simply strengthening her self-will, not her self-control. When training your child in self-control, remember the following:

1. Be resolved to win.
2. Don't take it personally.
3. Be consistent in your wording; keep it simple.
4. Be calm in manner and clear in your expectations.
5. Watch your child's attitude; correct a sour attitude.

Let us leave the idea of presenting "trees" of temptation with a fun example. We had a family devotion about resisting temptations with our children. Using the flannelgraph board, Tim told the story of Adam and Eve's temptation in the garden. He stressed the couple's feelings of longing as they walked by the fragrant fruit day after day. While Eve was considering taking the first bite of fruit, the children were shouting to the little felt figure: "Don't do it, Eve, eat a banana instead! Be strong; don't do it!" At the conclusion of the story, Kirsten introduced our own tree of temptation. She had taken a tabletop ivy topiary tree and taped little hard candies to it. We clearly instructed the children that, no matter what the circumstance or excuse, they were forbidden to take a piece of candy from the tree. We did not indicate that if they were good we would give them one. As time went by and we saw the children ignoring the tree, we would surprise them with a piece of hard candy from a jar in the kitchen. We were not cruelly teasing them with forbidden sweets; we were giving them sweet surprises for resisting temptation and exercising self-control.

When creating training scenarios such as this, it is important to be aware of your children's maturity level. Don't tempt them beyond their limits, frustrate them, and set them up for failure. Give your children appropriate opportunities to resist cravings and exercise their growing self-restraint and maturity. This teaching pays big dividends when you are visiting at someone else's home. Your children will be prepared to resist the tempting delights and will bring you honor by being told once not to touch. You will be invited back when your friends know that they will not have to sit on pins and needles while your little ones walk through their treasure-filled homes.

The Corral

While reading Laura Ingles Wilder's book, *Farmer Boy*, we were struck by the painstaking care with which ten-year-old Almanzo (Laura's eventual husband) trained his young oxen. He did not harness them, hitch them to a wagon, and drive them down the long road to town. He knew the distractions that town would inflict on his inexperienced team and how detrimental it would be to their long-term value in the field as plow animals. Instead, to begin their training, he yoked up his pair of oxen and simply drove them around the barnyard. Slowly and deliberately he walked behind his team, giving the commands "Gee" and "Haw," then gently directing them either right or left. He worked for hours giving these basic commands.[10]

Almanzo eventually tired of the repetitious task of training, and longed to take his team into the open fields. His wise father, who understood the basics of training, was there to oversee the whole process. The barnyard corral, he explained, was the perfect place to train his horses and oxen. In the stable the beasts would not have enough freedom of movement to maneuver and learn. On the other hand, the open prairie was without parameters and restrictions, and the animals would bolt, ignoring any instruction. The corral was restrictive enough to allow the trainer to correct mistakes while the training was in the first stages, where little rebellions and missteps were easily detected and corrected, and while the animals were young enough to learn a new habit.

So it is with training our children. It is a mistaken parenting philosophy that allows little ones to run freely, without boundaries, in the hope that their creativity will not be stifled. In the other extreme, the error is just as grave when the parent does not loosen the grip of control when a child has proven himself worthy of trust.

110% Effort at Home

We begin training our children in right behaviors and self-control from the earliest age. When the toddler, sitting contentedly on Daddy's lap, decides he wants to explore the floor and arches his back to slide down Daddy's leg to his destination, the lesson begins. You may say to yourself, "Wait a minute, toddler training? You have to be kidding." We aren't. If every time Junior grunts or whimpers his demands you jump to serve him, you are strengthening his self-indulgent will. The sooner your child training begins, the easier the process will be.

Let us clarify, we are not advocating denying food to a hungry baby or forcing him to be content in a swing for hours. No, indeed! We are encouraging you to look for little opportunities to proactively train your little one in self-control.

A wise couple, Michael and Debi Pearl in their book *To Train Up A Child*, calls these proactive training sessions 'Bootie Camp.'[11] Soldiers in military boot camp learn to subject their desires to the directions of their commanders, and to obey these directives without question, complaint, or delay. They work for days and weeks at immediate and precise response to leadership. They are neither coddled nor comforted. In fact, the sergeant almost delights in creating hardship for the new recruits, knowing that he is training them to face the real dangers of combat with the automatic right responses that may save their lives. In a similar manner we begin Bootie Camp as soon as our little guys can maneuver around the house.

The same principle is applied to sports. Michael Jordan once attributed his unprecedented success on the basketball court to the myriad hours of solitary practice far from his fans' adulation. He felt that if he gave practice 110% effort, the game would be easy. Indeed, he is famous for making the game look flawless and easy! The goal of Michael Jordan, and any athlete who strives for ultimate success, is to practice right behaviors so consistently that he does not have to think about them; they are automatic reflexes. In the pressure of the game, the right response is natural. If such concerted effort goes into success in the temporal world of professional athletics, how much more seriously should we approach preparing our children for right behaviors and success in the game of life?

> The more we train, the less we have to spank.

Practice, Practice, Practice

So, have we convinced you? Do you see the value of rehearsing right behaviors with your children? What right behaviors should you begin practicing? We work on our little ones coming to us when we call them one time, calmly and clearly; rehearsing cheerful and prompt responses and following parental (or any trusted adult in authority) directions. We do it with fun and games, and often surprise them with a small treat at the conclusion of a job well done.

We look for opportunities to interrupt our children when they are engrossed in an activity. For example, if our little girl is engrossed in constructing a building block kingdom, Kirsten calls, "McKenzie, come to Mommy."

"Just a minute, Mommy."

"No, honey. When Mommy calls you, you come immediately. Let's try it again."

"Yes, Ma'am."

She is instructed to go back to her blocks and at least act engrossed. "McKenzie, come to Mommy."

"Yes, Ma'am," she says, smiling and jumping up to obey.

"Good job, Girly-girl. Next time come the first time I call you," Kirsten says with a big, approving smile.

"Yes, Ma'am."

Kirsten then goes about her duties, allowing the child five or ten minutes to again become engrossed in being the princess of her wooden domain. "McKenzie, come to Mommy."

Up pops the little blonde head, "Yes, Ma'am." She flashes a self-satisfied smile.

"Wow! That was perfect. I need a hug from the sweetest three-year-old girl in the kingdom. Thank you for being so quick to obey."

Training for the Pew

More than once a worn-down mother or father has approached us after church and asked how we got our children to behave so well during the service. The secret is training at home! We would use read aloud time as a training session for right behavior in the pew. We would read aloud from good quality books without illustrations, encouraging the children to create pictures in their minds of what they heard. Before we picked up the book, we would read the portion of our church standards (included in the next chapter) that related to sitting and listening respectfully. We would stop and correct a child if he wiggled, talked, or distracted. We were mindful of their attention spans, not taxing them unduly beyond their capabilities. We rarely extended the sessions beyond 15 or 20 minutes when they were young. We rewarded a job well done by allowing them to quietly color or play with building blocks while we finished the chapter. Because of this consistent, proactive training at home, our little ones knew what we expected at church, and they were well prepared for it. As a consequence of training at home, there is much less need for correction at church, and services are enjoyable for all as a result.

Fun Drills

We would often do fun "drills" with all of the children. With everyone gathered in the family room for family time, possibly between chapters in a good book, or at a pause in a game, Tim would say, "Quick. Go touch the front door and come right back." "Yes, Sir," the chorus would cry as they leapt up to comply, knowing what fun the next few minutes would be.

"Now walk calmly to your bedrooms, turn on and off your light and walk back." "Yes, Sir."

"Yes, Sir."

"Yes, Sir."

We would smile as their giggles trailed off down the hall, knowing that in the midst of the fun, we were teaching our children the invaluable lessons of listening to instruction and of complying immediately, absolutely, and happily. "Good job, guys. Now go to the refrigerator and take out enough Popsicles® for everyone."

These training sessions are not in vain. In fact, they may save the life of your child. Knowing the dangers of running in shopping center parking lots, we taught our children to walk right with us. Holding hands as we walked to the store, we would surprise them with a calm, "Stop," expecting them to freeze on the spot. If they didn't respond immediately, we would take a moment to kindly admonish them and then proceed. "Stop." Everyone would come to a jerking halt. "Good job." And so the many practices would go.

Let us illustrate the life-saving value of this simple lesson. We were leaving the airport concourse after picking up a beloved auntie. Everyone was abuzz with excitement. Emily, then only four years old, darted out to the very edge of the busy airport pick-up lanes. "Stop." Emily stuck to the cement as she had been taught, just as a bulky delivery truck barreled by within inches of her. Had she not stopped, or had she even taken a few skipping steps before complying, she would have been crushed. Do not wonder if this is any exaggeration. She was literally inches from death. Both of us, shaken and tearful, embraced our frightened daughter,

Capitalize on the TEACHABLE MOMENTS

praising her for her instant obedience and then discussing the importance of instant obedience with the other children while we were all still shaken.

Lessons can be deeply learned and understood when these teachable moments occur. This opportunity provides the greatest impact when the "clay" is soft and pliable.

> **Your attitude determines your altitude.**
> – TR McDonald

Wimpy Goals

It is easy to become overwhelmed by the enormity of the task at hand. You may be thinking, every moment could be a teachable moment. If I spend all day training my children in all of these areas, when will there be time to do the laundry? Do not despair. Keep in mind that God never puts on us more than we are able to bear. And it is certainly not our intention to frustrate you. "Who hath despised the day of small things?" (Zechariah 4:10). A motivational and goal-setting speaker, Raymond Aaron, speaks about self-defeating attempts to change habits. He says that we often derail ourselves before we get out of the station by trying to tackle too many lofty goals at once. He recommends setting what he calls "wimpy goals."[12] Set one or two simple, attainable, quantifiable goals and work at those. Make your objectives simple and easy enough that success is attainable, especially in the beginning. Start with the basics; practice "Come to me," or do one fun drill per day until you feel successful, then move on. Success breeds success. Be encouraged by setting and reaching your daily goals. The rewards are well worth the effort!

Remember, it's SIMPLE...

• The first goal of Christian parenting is to teach our children self-control. We must train them to recognize evil, despise it, and choose to do right.

• It is to the profound benefit of our children that we provide opportunities inside our homes for self-control training, which will equip them for whatever enticements they face.

• This lesson is an incremental process. It requires the daily exercises of self-control, layered day upon day, month upon month, and year upon year...

• When training your child in self-control, remember the following:

- Be resolved to win.

- Don't take it personally.

- Be consistent in your wording; keep it simple.

- Be calm in manner and clear in your expectations.

- Watch your child's attitude; correct a sour attitude.

• Be careful. Don't tempt them beyond their limits, frustrate them, and set them up for failure. Give your children appropriate opportunities to resist cravings and exercise their growing self-restraint and maturity.

• Make 'bootie camp' fun.

• Train for the pew.

Chapter Six
RAISING THE STANDARD

The scene: Four-year-old Billy and his mother enter the grocery store to purchase a few items. Billy starts running laps around the navel orange display in the produce section.

"Now Billy, act right while we are in the store. Come here right now."

After a little game of catch-me-if-you-can, Mama corrals Billy and puts him in the shopping cart. While Mama is grabbing some cold cereal for tomorrow's breakfast, Billy begins punching the cereal boxes as though training for the championship fight.

"Billy, straighten up. You know how to behave."

Increasingly exasperated, Mother wheels Billy into the bread aisle. When Mama puts a loaf of sandwich bread into the cart, Billy grabs it and begins throwing it into the air like a football. He throws it higher and higher until Mama is certain that the good folks on aisle seven can see her bread in flight.

Mom shrieks, "Billy, knock that off! You are acting like a circus monkey." Frustrated and embarrassed,

Mother quickly completes her shopping and wheels Billy into the checkout lane. There he spots his favorite candy bar and the screaming begins…

Mama told Billy to "act right" and "straighten up," but does Billy know how to do this? Does he think that "straighten up" refers to his posture? Has Mom trained him in what is expected and proper in the store, at church, at the dinner table, when company comes, or when he visits others? Does he know what the consequences will be if he doesn't do right? The old adage, "If we fail to plan, we plan to fail," is very true when it comes to training our children.

It Is Written…

When God gave the Ten Commandments to the children of Israel in written form, there was no question or confusion about what He expected. There was no way to fudge or compromise or question; they simply looked again at the written words to be reminded of the standard. God, in fact, gave us 66 books that contain standards for our vertical relationship with Him, and for our horizontal relationships with each other. We know where to find the ways to please God; His instructions are clearly written in the Bible.

Likewise, parents and children need a written standard of expectation. It is easy to mistakenly assume our children know what we expect. When mama demands that Billy "straighten up" and "act right," she is not addressing specific actions. When there are no concrete expectations, Mama becomes frustrated and embarrassed, and Billy becomes frustrated and confused. The grocery store scene is not uncommon; it's what happens when we wait until we are in public and attempt to train our children "on the fly."

We have found that written standards of behavior, thoroughly taught, clearly trained, and consistently enforced, are effective in defusing much of the frustration in parenting. Standards of behavior are proactive rather than corrective. They are not arbitrary—the line is not constantly moving. They help to distinguish true disobedience from childish immaturity and foolishness. They develop self-control. Further, the process can be fun instead of frustrating.

Toddler Police

When our first children were young, we found ourselves saying "no" and "stop" much more than we wanted to and not saying "yes" enough. We felt like we were the toddler police, following the children around and correcting as they went on their merry way. We were *reacting* to their behaviors. We realized that we needed to be proactive. We began teaching the children what behaviors were right and acceptable, practicing them in fun family sessions, and reminding the children of what was expected before entering a situation. Becoming proactive became the most productive and rewarding element of our family training. We began to see positive results.

Standards provide a concrete expectation. They cannot be changed if Daddy is tired and does not feel like correcting or if Mommy is busy on the telephone. They are in force if friends are visiting or if the family is playing at the park. This consistency is good for both parents and children. We found that if we saw one of our children violating a standard, we were convicted to correct them because they knew their disobedience and they were aware that we knew it. We would discredit ourselves to turn a blind eye. It forced us to be consistent. It led them to anticipate correction when they knowingly did wrong and gave everyone a solid expectation.

How?

So what are these standards and how do we use them? Webster defines the word *standard* as "that which is established as a rule or model by the authority of respectable opinions or by custom and general consent." Our standards do not involve biblical doctrine or canon. They primarily spell out our behavior and manner expectations and examples. We began formulating these standards by taking note of all of the areas of behavior that needed specific training. We found that there were different sets of expectations for church, the store, when company was at our house or when we were visiting in other homes, as well as one set of general standards that were applicable everywhere. Then we began discussing and writing down the proper way to act in each setting. We formulated our standards from these lists. We worded our standards carefully. We wanted brief, kid-friendly mottos that would be easy for even the youngest child to memorize and remember. We wanted our verbal reminders to be affirmative, so we made the commands positive rather than negative. We tried to make each set as brief and descriptive as possible.

Once we were satisfied with our standards, we planned how we were going to introduce and implement them. We began on a family prayer night. We talked about the frustration of not having solid expectations and actually apologized to our children for the frustration that it may have caused them to be constantly corrected and not trained. Then we presented our standards. We did not bombard our little ones with list after list of do's and don'ts. We began with the area that was the most chaotic—church behavior—and then carefully timed the introduction of subsequent standards to avoid frustrating the children. We read the standards aloud, explaining what each one meant. We then acted out right behaviors as well as what was unacceptable. This became quite comical. In some areas we dressed up, acted up, and were generally silly. The children loved it. There was excitement and acceptance of our new family ways.

> A mother loves her child most divinely, not when she surrounds him with comfort, and anticipates his wants, but when she resolutely holds him to the highest standards and is content with nothing less than his best.
> – Hamilton Wright Nabie

In the ensuing years we have modified our standards only slightly. We now only say a few words or a phrase to remind the younger children that they are veering away from proper behavior. We keep a reduced-size copy of our standards in our day planner so that we can read them to the children on the way to church, or before we go into the store. Our table standards are posted by the dining table. The children say the standards along with us as we read.

Following are our standards with a few words of explanation. Your family may choose to use these verbatim or simply as a guideline for formulating your own. However you use them, it will not be a wasted exercise.

General Standards

> ➢ We will speak calmly and clearly one time. Look at us when we speak to you. We will know you hear and understand by a cheerful "Yes, Sir" or "Yes, Ma'am."

By far our most repeated and reminded standard. Every King has this one by heart. Now all Daddy has to say is, "We will speak..." and the choir joins the refrain, "calmly and clearly one time." Warning: you must be willing to chastise if you don't get cheerful obedience after one calm, clear directive. Remember, this is a commandment, not a suggestion; it must have consequences if violated.

The cheerful "Yes, Sir" or "Yes, Ma'am" is not only a symbol of respect that will serve them well in society, it is an attitude thermometer. If the mouth says "Yes, Sir" but the face says, "I am not happy with you right now, Daddy," or the feet stomp away, we know that we must deal swiftly and decisively with the attitude. A cheerful response also acknowledges that the child heard the parental directive. How often have you heard the excuse for not doing as you ask, "Daddy, I didn't hear you say that"? When they reply with a "Yes, Mommy," you know that they have heard you, have understood what you asked, and are now responsible to follow through.

➤ *Yes is yes: no is no. Lobbying, whining, and grumbling are not allowed.*

God dealt harshly with grumblers in the wilderness, lobbying employees don't last long in the workplace, and whining adults have few friends! Remember we are training our children to develop maturity. Let us teach them now that these tantrums are counter-productive.

➤ *Be respectful of adult conversations. Do not interrupt.*

This is a matter of respect for adults and requires developing self-control. We teach that there is only one acceptable way to approach adults in conversation, and we rehearse it at home. The child learns to discreetly reach up and gently squeeze Mom or Dad's arm and wait for a response. We wait for a natural break in the conversation and then address the child. An older child is capable of waiting longer than a little guy. Be aware of your children's attempts to be courteous and self-controlled. Answer them as soon as possible and always begin with a praise of their wonderful manners, "Thank you. You did a great job of waiting patiently. What do you need, Sweetie?" Exception: We do allow our children to interrupt in case of emergency (the desperate need of a candy bar is not an emergency).

> *Right is right; wrong is wrong. It is wrong to do the wrong thing for the right reasons. Our moral code does not change.* (Probably the most important one on the list!)

> *If it's not fun for all, it's not fun at all! Do unto others, as you would have them do unto you. Do not be unkind and call it joking. Be considerate of everyone's feelings and viewpoints even if they are different from yours.*

This is another King family motto. Overt bullying is not allowed under any circumstances. Teasing and joking are only subtle forms of bullying and cruelty. Adolph Hitler was a bully. "As a mad man who casteth firebrands, arrows, and death, so is the man that deceiveth his neighbor, and saith, Am not I in sport?" (Proverbs 26:18, 19) The NIV says it like this, "Like a madman shooting firebrands or deadly arrows, is a man who deceives his neighbor and says, 'I was only joking!'" Simply put, we do not allow fun

> **If it's not fun for all, it's not fun at all!**

at someone else's expense. If it's not fun for all, it's not fun at all!

> *If you need to speak to us, come to us, do not expect us to come to you. We do not hear yelling.*

This is another facet of respect for parents and demand for self-control. It also cuts down on the cacophony of noises in our home!

> *Rejoice with them that rejoice, mourn with them that mourn. Remember that we are a team! We will only succeed when we all pull together, work together, stand up for one another, stick together!*

We are always looking for ways to teach our children this real-world principle.

Church Standards

Remember that these are our personal standards. They can serve as guidelines for you. They have evolved over the years into standards that teach love and respect for the house of God, the pastor, our neighbors, and each other while at church. Church is fun. We love to exuberantly worship God and encourage our children to do the same.

WE WORSHIP TOGETHER

> *Sing, clap, stand, and raise your hands when Mom and Dad do.*

> *Juke and jive if you want to. Be appropriate.*

WE LOVE AND RESPECT GOD'S HOUSE

> *Before and after church, we are eagles.*

We have taught our children that eagles are regal birds that live high above the common areas, soaring alone, and that, like eagles, sometimes they may have to fly alone in the face of others doing things that we don't do. We do not do this to teach our children to feel superior to their peers. Instead, we want them to understand and identify with a symbol of strength that is often alone because it can reach higher heights than most birds. We love word pictures, and we want to picture a bright future for our children; we want them to know that being the only one doing the right thing is always cool, regardless of what others think. Didn't someone say, "It's hard to soar with the eagles when you run with the turkeys"? We teach our children to soar away from the turkeys when they try to drag the eagles down.

➤ *Be quiet, respectful, and attentive during preaching, prayers, and testimonies. No talking, turning around, or disrespect.*

➤ *No running, wrestling or roughhousing.*

➤ *Go to the bathroom before church.*

➤ *Do not ask anyone for candy.* We are not training panhandlers.

➤ *Look for opportunities to minister to others, both young and old, through prayer, a kind word or deed.*

Table Standards

It is important to us that dinnertime be a family fun time, so we try not to do our table manners training at the dinner table. We work at these standards at lunchtime (we home school our children, so this may not be an option for you), and try out our skills at the dinner table. We begin most dinners with the reading of our table standards, a simple reminder of our expectations. We do not generally chastise for "manners" infractions during dinner, preferring to remind with humor. When someone forgets to put their napkin on their lap, they must walk to the front door, touch it, come back to the table, put their napkin on their lap, and continue with the meal. If we catch anyone open-mouth chewing or finger-licking (and it's not southern fried chicken), we have the child stand behind his or her chair for two minutes. If you are diligent with the other standards, vigilance about table standards during dinner will not be necessary; just reading and explaining them to the children with reminders before dinnertime should suffice.

> *Always come neat and clean to the dinner table. Wash hands and face, comb hair, and wear clean clothes.*

> *Wait patiently with your hands in your lap for everyone to be seated.*

> *Use good posture at the table. Sit without slouching, leaning on the table with your elbows or tilting your chair back on two legs.*

> *Put your napkin on your lap.*

> *Be respectful of everyone's prayers and conversation.*

> *Always wait until your mother or the hostess starts eating before you begin.*

There are few things more frustrating for a mother than finally sitting down at the dinner table to realize that everyone but the baby has finished eating. To show consideration and respect for Kirsten (or the hostess, should we be in someone else's home), we all wait until everyone is served their entire meal and until Mommy takes her first bite of food before the rest of the family begins eating. It shows deference to the hostess, exercises everyone's self-restraint, and allows the family to enjoy the meal together.

> ➤ *Eat everything you are given with a thankful attitude. Take only as much food as you know you will eat, and then be sure to eat what you take.*

> ➤ *Eat neatly and silently. Take small bites and chew with your mouth closed. Swallow before speaking. Keep one hand in your lap. Use a pusher, not a finger.*

> ➤ *You may ask to be excused in your own home but not in restaurants or while visiting others. Thank the cook, find something to compliment, take your own plate to the sink, and help with kitchen cleanup.*

Store Standards

Our general standards are in effect at all times. No whining or begging is acceptable in the store as well as at home. If Mama says no candy, nothing less than a cheerful "Yes, Mama" is acceptable. However, the grocery store is not—we repeat, not—the place to introduce these things. Home, where you can swiftly and decisively mete out the correction for crying and whining, is the first place to master the basics of self-control. Only after we feel confident at home, we make a trip to the grocery store to exercise our new standards. We do not go with an exhaustive, full month's shopping list. We go the first few times with the express reason to train in-store standards; we do our big shopping without the little ones.

> ## Private victories precede public victories
> – Stephen R. Covey

Sitting in the parking lot, we read the store standards that we keep in our day planner or in the car. The children clearly know what to expect. We have been known to leave our cart half filled with groceries to go home and discipline a child for a blatant violation of our standards. It only takes an incident or two of follow-through for the child to know that Mother means business! Proactive training at home, consistent expectations, and calm, resolute correction for violations will translate into order and peace wherever you go with your child.

> *Walk and stay with Mom or Dad. Keep one hand on cart. Do not run or wander.*

> *Keep your hands together or in your pockets. Do not touch anything unless asked to help or given permission. This is used if we are in a store or situation with no shopping carts or stroller.*

> *Use a quiet voice. Say things one time and wait for a response.* Mom is often in thought in the store ("Do we have spaghetti noodles at home? I forgot to look."), and it is easy not to hear the first few calls of, "Mommy... Mommy...Moooooommmmmeeeeee...." We teach the children to wait patiently or to use our general interruption arm squeeze to gain our attention.

> *Do not point or stare at people's differences. Compliment something about them.*

> *Look people in the eye when they talk to you. Say thank you when you are complimented.*

> *Look for ways to help your mother and father, or others.*

Billy, Revisited

After a few weeks of training in some simple store standards, Mama again took Billy to the grocery store. She reminded him of her expectations by reading them before they left the car. They took a cart and a short grocery list and embarked on a new and refreshing experience.

Billy kept his hand on the shopping cart. When Mother asked him to grab a loaf of bread, Billy cheerfully obeyed. When they had finished picking up all the items on their list without incident and pulled into the checkout lane, Mama complimented Billy on his excellent behavior and surprised him with a piece of his favorite candy. Their mutual hard work had paid off. Both Billy and Mama were proud of their improvement.

God gave His people a written Word to follow. We are reminded of it through the preaching of the Word. Billy's mother decided to follow God's example and give her son solid structure. An explicit system with a clear direction and a method of being reminded created order and peace for both Mom and Billy, as well as all who were in the grocery store!

Following are our complete, brief standards. You may copy, or adapt them to your family:

General Standards

> ➤ We will speak calmly and clearly one time. Look at us when we speak to you. We will know you hear and understand by a cheerful "Yes, Sir" or "Yes, Ma'am."

> ➤ Yes is yes: no is no. Whining, lobbying, and grumbling are not allowed.

> ➤ Be respectful of adult conversations. Do not interrupt.

> ➤ Right is right; wrong is wrong. It is wrong to do the wrong thing for the right reasons. Our moral code does not change.

> ➤ If it's not fun for all, it's not fun at all! Do not be unkind and call it joking. Be considerate of everyone's feelings and viewpoints even if they are different from yours.

➤ If you need to speak to us, come to us, do not expect us to come to you. We do not hear yelling.

➤ Rejoice with them that rejoice, mourn with them that mourn. Remember that we are a team! We will only succeed when we all pull together, work together, stand up for one another, stick together!

Church Standards

WE WORSHIP TOGETHER

➤ Sing, clap, stand, and raise your hands when Mom and Dad do.

➤ Juke and jive if you want to. Be appropriate.

WE LOVE AND RESPECT GOD'S HOUSE

➤ Before and after church, we are eagles.

➤ Be quiet, respectful, and attentive during preaching, prayers, and testimonies. No talking, turning around, or disrespect.

➤ No running, wrestling or roughhousing.

➤ Go to the bathroom before church.

➤ Do not ask anyone for candy.

➤ Look for opportunities to minister to others, both young and old, through prayer, a kind word or deed.

Table Standards

➤ Always come neat and clean to the dinner table.

➤ Wash hand and face, comb hair, and wear clean clothes.

➤ Wait patiently with your hands in your lap for everyone to be seated.

- Use good posture at the table. Sit without slouching, leaning on the table with your elbows or tilting your chair back on two legs.

- Put your napkin on your lap.

- Be respectful of everyone's prayers and conversation.

- Always wait until your mother or the hostess starts eating before you begin.

- Eat everything you are given with a thankful attitude.

- Take only as much food as you know you will eat, and then be sure to eat what you take.

- Eat neatly and silently. Take small bites and chew with your mouth closed, swallow before speaking, keep one hand in your lap. Use a pusher, not a finger.

- You may ask to be excused in your own home but not while visiting others. Thank the cook, find something to compliment, take your own plate to the sink, and help with kitchen cleanup.

Store Standards

- Walk and stay with Mom or Dad.

- Keep one hand on cart.

- Do not run or wander.

- Keep your hands together or in your pockets or on the shopping cart. Do not touch *anything* unless asked to help or given permission.

- Use a quiet voice. Say things one time and wait for a response.

- Do not point or stare at people's differences.

Compliment something about them.

> Look people in the eye when they talk to you. Say thank you when you are complimented.

> Look for ways to help your mother and father, or others.

Remember, it's SIMPLE...

• God's instructions are clearly written in the Bible. When God gave the Ten Commandments to the children of Israel in written form, there was no question or confusion about what He expected.

• Likewise, parents and children need a written standard of expectation. We have found that written standards of behavior, thoroughly taught, clearly trained, and consistently enforced, are effective in defusing much of the frustration in parenting.

• Standards of behavior are proactive rather than corrective. Standards provide a concrete expectation. This consistency is good for both parents and children. It forces us to be consistent. It leads the children to anticipate correction when they knowingly did wrong and gives everyone a solid expectation.

• Our written standards primarily spell out our behavior and manner expectations and examples.

HOW?

FORMULATION

• We began formulating these standards by taking note of all of the areas of behavior that needed specific training.

• Then we began discussing and writing down the proper way to act in each setting.

• We worded our standards carefully. We wanted brief, kid-friendly mottos that would be easy for even the youngest child to memorize and remember.

• We made the commands positive rather than negative. We tried to make each set as brief and descriptive as possible.

IMPLEMENTATION

• We began on a family prayer night.

• We apologized to our children for the frustration that it may have caused them to be constantly corrected and not trained.

• Then we began with our church standards because church behavior was our area of greatest immediate need.

• We read the standards aloud, explaining what each one meant.

• We then acted out right behaviors as well as what was unacceptable.

• We have modified our standards only slightly.

• We keep a reduced-size copy of our standards with us or in our day planner for quick reminders.

Chapter Seven
DELIGHT!

*Y*ou have seen the "All Rules" family. The children practically march in line, remain silent at all times, and seem to be veritable automatons. They flinch at the sound of their father's snarling voice. He berates them in public, calling them stupid, useless, and failures. Their eyes are lackluster; they seem withdrawn and dull, but, boy, do they behave. They sit through church without much response, and once outside the sanctuary doors they teeter on the edge of rebellion and flirting with the world. What you do not see is the silent tension that reigns in their home. Everyone lives in fear of aggravating Dad or Mom, which doesn't take much. Meals are eaten in silence because "Children should be seen and not heard." The oldest child counts the months until he turns 18, planning to leave any way he can.

You have no doubt run into, or been run over by, the "All Relationship" family. You try not to sit near them in church, knowing that you will get nothing from the message with their little boy making faces at your children and lobbing crayons over the pew. They talk, fight, bounce, and squeal unashamedly throughout the service. Eating with them makes even the strongest of stomachs queasy. You have been keeping your son by your side after church since their son threatened to "take him outside and teach him a lesson." You are "busy" the day they invite your family to the zoo with them, knowing how embarrassing and unpredictable their children can be in public. They laugh loudly, run and cavort unrestrainedly, and have very few rules or manners.

Balancing Act

Both families, admittedly exaggerated to make our point, are sorely out of balance. Some wise student of human nature (we wish we could remember who!) offered a simple law concerning family interaction:

All Rules + no Relationship = Rebellion

All Relationship + no Rules = Chaos

The solution to the extreme nature of these equations is balance. The Webster's definition of balance is "to adjust the weights in the scales of a balance so as to bring them to equipoise. Hence, to regulate different powers so as to keep them in a state of proportion." When we focus too heavily on the side of rules, to the neglect of relationship, the bond with our children is strained. Conversely, when we generate fun, fun, fun, making life one big party without setting much-needed parameters for our children, pandemonium ensues.

So much of our focus as parents is on training and discipline. "Make your bed." "Do your homework." "Sit up straight at the dinner table." "Go back in and brush your teeth again, young man." "Stop." "Don't." And so it continues in a seemingly endless chant of correction and reminders. While it is right and necessary to disciple our children in the paths of righteousness, responsibility, and maturity, all correction and no connection can make Jack a resentful boy! There must be a critical balance struck between rules and relationship. We must consciously and deliberately nurture relationship with our children daily. We can begin by showing visible delight in our children, which is an everyday habit that will reap benefits and blessings for a lifetime!

Can't Buy Me Love

Many years ago we read a newspaper article in which a federal drug enforcement agent made a profound observation that sobered us and drove us to diligence in nurturing close relationships with each of our sons and daughters. When asked why children become embroiled in drugs and gangs even at young ages, he replied that these children are looking for love and acceptance. He assured parents that if they did not consciously cultivate strong connections with their young people, they would "lose their children to the first person who [told] them that they [were] special." The world is full of voices eager to tell our children how special they are if we neglect to. Ironically, the federal agent made no mention of material possessions. He did not say that children turned to drugs because they lacked "stuff." The size of the children's house or the style or relative cost of their sneakers never factored into their turn to illegal and self destructive habits.

It's true, the acquisition of "things" does not factor into a child's ultimate sense of approval and self-worth. Many parents erroneously feel that gifting their children with whatever they desire equates with love and relieves them of the duty of spending time with their needy offspring. However, children are aware of our guilty attempts to purchase affection through gifts of money or trinkets. We have heard the pain of adults who, as children, were handed money and gifts in lieu of affection by well-meaning but guilt-ridden parents. They remember that their cravings for a loving touch and their longings for an approving smile were never satisfied. The dearth of loving connection was intensified, not abated, by the giving of comparatively cheap and meaningless material offerings. There is no substitute for a parent's loving attention.

Unlike the luster of a shiny, new bike that will soon rust or the joy of a dolly that eats, talks, and cries whose beauty will fade, affectionate bonds of love neither rust nor fade. The gifts that will live on in fond memories and in the developing character of our children are the gifts of loving touches, delighted smiles, meaningful conversations, and joyful laughter. We have sprinkled these ideas throughout the book; however, because we feel so strongly the need to balance rules with relationship, we have devoted this chapter to that single subject. We want parents to be aware of the vital impact that time spent delighting in their children will have, both now and into adulthood.

Bind us together, Lord!

In church we often sing a song of unity that powerfully illustrates our goal of relationship with our children:

> *Bind us together, Lord, Bind us together,*
> *With cords that cannot be broken.*
> *Bind us together, Lord, Bind us together, Lord,*
> *Bind us together with love.*

The word picture is beautiful. Love is likened to cords that encircle two people, joining them together so strongly that the bond cannot be severed. How do such cords become entwined around these two? By love. Not the emotional pitter-pat of the heart that inconsistently runs hot and cold. This bonding love is patient, kind, does not envy, is not proud, doesn't seek its own. It is others-minded, it is not easily provoked, and it thinks no evil. This love bears all things, believes all things, hopes all things, and endures all things according to the ultimate discourse on love found in 1 Corinthians 13. You may ask, wouldn't such terms be lost on a child? How will he understand such nebulous and intangible expressions? He will see them through your actions. When you smile approvingly at him, he will feel the soft, silkiness of a cord of love slip around his heart, binding him to you. When you take the time to truly listen and laugh at last night's incredibly strange dream, he will sense some invisible tugging that draws him closer to you. When you hug him close after a disappointment, the velvety yet tough strand of love will bind you closer still. When you stop a frenzied rush because he needs you, you are knitting your hearts together. It is extraordinary and almost magical to sense the bonds growing stronger. Remember that tying cords of fellowship is the counterbalance to discipline and training. It is vital to maintain equilibrium between the two.

> Remember that tying cords of fellowship is the counterbalance to discipline and training.

How?

"Oh, I am convicted. I realize that I've rushed past so many opportunities. Is it too late?" Never! That is the exciting news. Children are resilient. Because they so crave this kind of loving affection, they will respond fairly quickly. Some tough nuts may take a little more perseverance. You must resolve to continue to wear away the resistance. "So what do I do?" If you are still a bit mystified by the idea, invest in one of the 1000 Ways to Tell Your Child You Love Him type of book. There are dozens of them. We are sure that they will stir your sentimental juices. Here are a few ideas to get you started:

> Say, "I love you," often. They can never hear it too much!

> Write encouraging notes and tuck them in unexpected places. Tim and our daughters have this one down to perfection. Emily has a shoe box full of the notes she and her daddy have passed back and forth since she was old enough to draw a heart and sign her name. McKenzie has now caught the bug, and is surprising and being surprised by her daddy's valued love notes.

> Be big enough to say, "I'm sorry," if you have wronged your child.

> Touch your children meaningfully. Gary Smalley and John Trent discuss the value of meaningful touch as a means of transferring worth and blessing to one's children in their best-seller, The Blessing, a healing book for those adults who did not receive meaningful touches from their own parents. They state, "At times, the smallest act of touch can be a vehicle to communicating love and personal acceptance."[13] Dad, do you know how important it is for you to hug your son or daughter? Giving your children meaningful

> If you talk to your children, you can help them keep their lives together. If you talk to them skillfully, you can help them to build future dreams.
>
> – Jim Rohn

touches and hugs is like giving withered plants water or healthy plants fertilizer. Don't stop giving them loving affection when they are teenagers; this is an important time of consistently binding them to you with cords of love.

➤ Picture a bright future for your child. Smalley and Trent state, "When a person feels in his or her heart that the future is hopeful and something to look forward to, it can greatly affect his or her attitude on life."[14] When you speak of a bright future for your child, he believes you, senses your belief in him, and strives harder. Remember that "faith is the substance of things hoped for, the evidence of things not seen" (Heb. 11:1). The picture of a bright future that you develop in your mind for your children translates into your words of encouragement, conversations that inspire, and a resolve in your son or daughter to do great things. Take a few minutes to re-read the "Eight Cow Wife" in chapter two and apply the concept to your family.

➤ Listen—take genuine concern in their interests.

➤ Take dates with each child individually. In our family these are generally called "doughnut dates." Over the years when Tim has felt the need to connect with one of the children, he has surprised them with a doughnut date. It costs $3, and its dividends exceed multiple millions! It's a great investment.

➤ Read together. Whether snuggling together as a twosome or as a family flopped all over the living room, read-aloud sessions are some of our most precious memories and "cord-tiers." We will expand on the value of reading aloud in the following few chapters. Suffice it to say here, however, that it is so rewarding!

➤ Sing special songs to your children. Use their name in the songs if possible. Nothing is as sweet as hearing your name sung by a loving daddy or mama.

> The best inheritance a person can give to his children is a few minutes of his time each day.
> – O.A. Battista

Kirsten wakes the children every Sunday morning with a rousing chorus of "Everybody ought to go to Sunday school" replacing "the men, and the women, the boys and the girls" with our children's names. Corny? Maybe. But it's not Sunday morning without it.

➤ Wrestle, play, tickle, giggle, laugh, chase each other…just delight!

Again, this is by no means an exhaustive list, but a jump-start. No one knows your children like you do. You know their love language, the displays of affection that are most meaningful to them. Ponder and plan, then sow and reap. Oh, what a sweet and rewarding crop!

Broken Cords

If small acts of love bind us together, what is the result of disapproving or insensitive acts? Why, the opposite, of course. As easy as it is to draw our children to us by simple acts of kindness and thoughtfulness, we can drive them from us by subtle displeasure and dissatisfaction. While we cannot expect to always be positive and uplifting and to never show exasperation with our children, we must be sure to spend more time binding ourselves together than severing the cords of fellowship. There are a few ways of provoking our children that are more damaging (not to mention reprehensible) than others. Let us take a few minutes to warn you against these counterproductive activities.

➤ Verbally abusing them. Using derogatory terms such as stupid, idiot, good-for-nothing, etc. This is picturing a dismal future for them by name-calling. Children will become what you prophesy for them. "Death and life are in the power of the tongue" (Prov. 18:21). Words are life or death. Words create; God spoke and the worlds were made.

➤ Embarrassing them. Publicly discussing their weaknesses, belittling them, laughing at their expense. Making fun of any physical oddity: "Skinny," "Bucky," "Dumbo", etc.

➤ Teasing and bullying. Hitler was bullied as a boy and became one of history's most notorious bullies. Only a weak person picks on those smaller than himself. Such behavior is devastating for a child to suffer at the hand of a parent, the very person who should be protecting him from such heinous behavior. Remember our standard: if it's not fun for all, it's not fun at all. Even tickling or wrestling until the child is angry or frustrated is bullying. We have worked out a catch phrase to stop horseplay from becoming out of hand. When anyone says, "I'm not having fun," the activity stops immediately. This way we avoid provoking each other to anger.

➤ Venting your anger on your child. This is really a matter of self-control on the part of the parent.

➤ Harsh lecturing and inconsistent discipline.

➤ Being a hypocrite—being unwilling to do and be what you expect of them. Holding them to a double standard.

That parents would purposely do any of the above is beyond our comprehension. They need an altar of repentance, the empowering Spirit of God to help them to change, and the resolve to do so. But not everyone who severs cords does so intentionally. Sometimes we inadvertently yet negatively affect our children through our habits. Pause now and reflect. Are you unwittingly provoking your child to anger? Remember Ephesians 6:4, "And, ye fathers, provoke not your children to wrath: but bring them up in the nurture and admonition of the Lord."

> Our children are watching us live, and what we are shouts louder than anything we can say.
> – Wilfred A. Peterson

Mama, Are You Mad?

A dear friend, who is an exemplary mother, related a surprising conversation she had with one of her children that revealed to her the importance of a simple smile. Her children would ask, "Mommy, are you mad?" or "Mommy, do you feel okay? You look upset," or "Mama, have I done something to upset you?"

Frustrated by their frequent interrogations, and sensing their insecurity, she stopped one day and asked one of them why they constantly questioned her about her ill mood. The answer surprised and sobered this good and loving mother.

"Mama, you always look so mad. We think that you are angry with us."

"I'm not mad, honey. Why do you think I look so mad?"

"Your face always looks so serious. You just look angry."

She pondered the girl's answer and tried to be conscious of her facial expressions throughout the following days. She realized that she habitually frowned or had a sullen countenance. She was not at all mad, but focused and absorbed in her own thoughts or activities. It was easy to see, however, why her children thought she was angry. Even her resting facial expression was a serious one. She decided to give concerted effort to changing that habit. She is now working toward the goal of an unconscious, natural, smiling countenance, and happily reports that the tension in her home is greatly diminished! There is power in a smile.

> A smile is the lighting system of the face,
> The cooling system of the head,
> And the heating system of the heart.
> – Unknown

A Delightful Definition

So, again, what does it mean to delight in our children? A source of delight is "that which gives great pleasure, a high degree of satisfaction. Delight is a more permanent pleasure than joy, and not dependent on sudden excitement." Delight does not require fireworks or a dozen red roses. Instead of the spectacular, it depends on the simple to create that high degree of satisfaction. The Bible tells us in many places that God delights in His upright, truthful, prayerful, righteous children (Proverbs 8:30; 11:20; 12:22; 15:8). Similarly, we must be sure that our actions and attitudes reflect the delight of our souls; our children need to recognize our delight in them. Hugging, patting, hand holding, even hair ruffling are small but significant tokens of fondness and approval. Smiling conveys your appreciation and support without a word. The delight your daughter sees reflected in your smile "fills her cup" of self-worth and confidence. When you listen intently to your son, he feels that you value his thoughts. He can sense how genuinely valuable he is to you. Laughing with your children binds you together as nothing else will. Laugh until you cry and snort! Sit by the fire, drink hot cocoa, eat popcorn, laugh, and nurture your family. Become bound together with silken cords of love. We are the first expression of Jesus that our children will know. What will we teach them about our loving Daddy? Will they know that they can run into His arms or will they be timid and afraid? Our joy and delight will make the difference!

We are the first expression of Jesus that our children will know. What will we teach them about our loving Daddy? Will they know that they can run into His arms or will they be timid and afraid? Our joy and delight will make the difference!

Smile

Kirsten has a goal that might sound a bit crazy at first. She wants "smiley wrinkles." Over the past number of years, we have conducted a very unscientific study on smiling. We have observed that you can infer the countenance and attitude a person has had throughout life by the lines that time has etched on his face. In coffee shops, mall settings, or any public place, we have observed elderly people, noticing their wrinkle patterns, and deciding whether they have spent more time smiling or frowning. (Remember we said that this was a very unscientific observation.) We would make our initial guess at their disposition, and then watch their facial expressions for a few minutes. More often than not, a person who has wrinkles that turn down and that give them a generally sad or irritated look, act that way as well. On the other hand, the person who has smiley wrinkles—you know her, the grandmotherly woman with the upturned creases around her twinkling eyes and cheery mouth—will be generally pleasant to those with whom she interacts.

Face it. Every one of our faces will crease and crinkle as we age. We want smiley wrinkles, don't you?

The secret is you must start now!

Smile!

May 27, 1996
Dear Daddy,

I Love you. You are a good daddy. Sometimes you help me with school. I am happy that you are my daddy. I love you very very much. I like when you take me to Cassidy's and we sit outside. You are the best daddy in the whole world. Thank you for the letter you wrote to me today. I love you with all my heart, and your hugs and kisses are the best. Thank you for my great daddy in the whole world. I am praying for you to be the best daddy. Thank you for working in school and work. I really love you for all the things you have given me. God gave me the best daddy. God is good. He made my daddy and I love you.

Your little girl,
Emily
Age 7

Delightful Words of Wisdom

Flatter me, and I may not believe you.
Criticize me, and I may not like you.
Ignore me, and I may not forgive you.
Encourage me, and I will not forget you.
William Arthur Ward

———

Self-esteem is so delicate a flower
that praise tends to make it bloom,
while discouragement often nips it in the bud.
Alex. F. Osborn

———

Listen a hundred times,
Ponder a thousand times,
Speak once!

———

If your vision is for a year, plant flowers.
If your vision is for ten years, plant trees.
If your vision is for a lifetime, plant people.

Remember, it's SIMPLE...

- All Rules + No Relationship = Rebellion
  All Relationship + No Rules = Chaos

- All correction and no connection can make Jack a resentful boy! There must be a critical balance struck between rules and relationship.

- We must consciously and deliberately nurture relationship with our children daily.

- If parents do not consciously cultivate strong connections with their young people, they will "lose their children to the first person who [told] them that they [were] special."

- The acquisition of "things" does not factor into a child's ultimate sense of approval and self-worth. Many parents erroneously feel that gifting their children with whatever they desire equates with love and relieves them of the duty of spending time with their needy offspring.

- Tying cords of fellowship is the counterbalance to discipline and training.

- Be creative, individual and consistent in showing each child your loving attention.

- We must be sure to spend more time binding ourselves together than severing the cords of fellowship. There are a few ways of provoking our children that are more damaging (not to mention reprehensible) than others. Let us take a few minutes to warn you against these counterproductive activities.

- Delight depends on the simple to create that high degree of satisfaction. A source of delight is "that which gives great pleasure, a high degree of satisfaction. Delight is a more permanent pleasure than joy, and not dependent on sudden excitement." Delight does not require fireworks or a dozen red roses.

• We should look for ways to display our delight in our children every day, filling their cups of confidence and self-worth.

PART TWO

HELPING YOUR CHILD
Become...

WISE

Chapter Eight
A WORD
TO THE WISE

*A*t the onset of this book we established the goal of child training as nurturing our children to a state of full development or readiness for adult life through godly intellectual, practical, moral, and spiritual training. We asserted that the scope of child training falls into three major areas: self-control, wisdom, and responsibility. Let us now turn our attention to the aspect of instruction in godly wisdom.

A Wise Definition

What is wisdom? Wisdom is the structure for successful Christian living. It is the ability to learn from experiences and make sound decisions. It is godly understanding and insight. Wisdom requires acting with Christian character. In his original 1828 dictionary Daniel Webster defines wisdom as follows: "The right use or exercise of knowledge; the choice of laudable ends, and of the best means to accomplish them. This is wisdom in *act, effect,* or *practice.* If wisdom is to be considered as a faculty of the mind, it is the faculty of discerning or judging what is most just, proper and useful, and if it is to be considered as an *acquirement*, it is the knowledge and use of what is best, most just, most proper, most conducive to prosperity or happiness." Our simple definition of wisdom is "knowledge rightly applied."

> Our simple definition of wisdom is knowledge rightly applied.

You may ask, When should we begin godly instruction? Should we wait until our children demonstrate a modicum of self-discipline? No! Do not delay! Start today. Remember Proverbs 22:15 says, "Foolishness is bound up in the heart of a child..." and Psalm 58:3 says that "the wicked are estranged from the womb: they go astray as soon as they be born, speaking lies." The promises to the foolish and wicked are poverty, despair, death, and hell. However, the Bible promises that "by humility and the fear the Lord are riches, and honor, and life" (Proverbs 22:4). It is possible to begin instilling wisdom in our children before they are completely self-controlled; these lessons should be taught simultaneously. Again, true wisdom takes time and requires growing self-government. It is never too early to begin instilling a love for God, His Word, His ways and people.

Sweet Tooth

Proverbs 22:6 instructs parents to "train up a child in the way he should go: and when he is old, he will not depart from it." We once heard it explained that the Hebrew root word for *to train up* is the same word for "the palate, the roof of the mouth, or gums." At first glance, this meaning may not seem relevant to the Scripture, but it contains an interpretation worth exploring. Upon the birth of a child in King Solomon's day, midwives would dip a cloth in the juice of crushed dates and massage the gums and palate of newborn infants in order to stimulate the sucking reflex, preparing the newborn to nurse. They were training the taste of the infants to the nutrients necessary to sustain their young lives. In like manner, we are to introduce the sweet nectar of God while our newborn children are developing their tastes and appetites, and when they are old, no counterfeit the world might offer them will taste as sweet as what Daddy and Mama have been feeding them since birth.

It is natural to feel a bit overwhelmed at the daunting task of teaching our children in the ways of godly wisdom. But fear not! Instruction in wisdom will not be accomplished in one sitting or even in one year. It is a process. We must look at wisdom as a never-ending lesson; it begins in infancy and ends with our last breaths. If we are honest with ourselves, we

> As we coach our children in wisdom, they are teaching us more than a few lessons in the subject.

will admit that *we* are still growing in wisdom. As we coach our children in wisdom, they are teaching us more than a few lessons in the subject! Although the depth and layers of instructing in wisdom change as our children grow, there are methods and means as well as times and opportunities that can be used with any child at any age.

The King's Advice

If you are feeling unequal to the task of imparting godly wisdom, let us share something that has helped us greatly through the years. Conveniently, God's book of wisdom, Proverbs, has 31 chapters. Many years ago, on the advice of a dear and wise father-in-the-Lord, we began reading one chapter of Proverbs each day. As we read, we asked the Lord for the wisdom that He had promised to give liberally. We discovered that much of life's trials, complexities, and situations are addressed therein. Try beginning each day with a chapter of God's wisdom and a prayer for understanding. He will respond by blessing you with both wisdom and confidence. Take a moment to read the following promises of blessing to the wise, and the promises of ruin to the foolish from the Book of Proverbs. See how the wisest man in history actively leads his own son in the ways of wisdom and life and warns him against the snares of folly.

The fear of the LORD is the beginning of knowledge, but fools despise wisdom and discipline (1:7).

For the turning away of the simple shall slay them, and the prosperity of fools shall destroy them. But whoso hearkeneth unto me shall dwell safely, and shall be quiet from fear of evil (1:32, 33).

My son, if thou wilt receive my words, and hide my commandments with thee; so that thou incline thine ear unto wisdom, and apply thine heart to understanding; yea, if thou criest after knowledge, and liftest up thy voice for understanding, if thou seekest her as silver and searchest for her as for hid treasures; then shall thou understand the fear of the lord, and find the knowledge of God. For the lord giveth wisdom: out of his mouth cometh knowledge and understanding; He layeth up sound wisdom for the righteous: he is a buckler to them that walk uprightly (2:1-8)

My son, forget not my law; but let thine heart keep my commandments: For length of days, and long life, and peace, shall they add to thee (3:1, 2).

The wise shall inherit glory: but shame shall be the promotion of fools (3:35).

Get wisdom, get understanding: forget it not; neither decline from the words of my mouth. Forsake her not, and she shall preserve thee; love her, and she shall keep thee. Wisdom is the principal thing; therefore get wisdom: and with all thy getting get understanding; Exalt her, and she shall promote thee; she shall bring thee to honour, when thou dost embrace her. She shall give to thine head an ornament of grace; a crown of glory shall she deliver to thee (4: 5 –9).

The proverbs of Solomon. A wise son maketh a glad father; but a foolish son is the heaviness of his mother (10:1).

He that walketh with wise men shall be wise: but a companion of fools shall be destroyed (13:20).

Personality vs. Character

Let us take a moment to make an important distinction between character and personality. When we discuss training our children in the ways of godly wisdom, we are talking about guiding and training their characters. Character denotes moral strength and virtue; it is honesty, integrity, trustworthiness, kindness, faithfulness, diligence, perseverance, and so on. We must be diligent observers of our children, watching for evidences of their growing characters. Their tone, patience, and kindness when speaking to others, decisions they make, friends they gravitate towards, their willingness to be helpful, what they do when faced with temptation, and such similar situations will show how their characters are shaping.

Character is not to be confused with personality, distinctive qualities, or skills and talents that make each individual unique. We must be aware of and avoid the pitfall of trying to bend our child's personality while neglecting his character. Some children are naturally charming and gregarious, joking and enlivening the atmosphere wherever they go. Others are tranquil and reflective, preferring to be observers rather than participants in the games and pranks children play. Talents vary: some are musical, athletic, literary, mathematical, oratorical, socially adept, mechanical, and so on. An athletic dad must value his son's mechanical ability, and respect his choice of tinkering with car engines over football scrimmages. If a daughter does not have the voice of a nightingale, a musically gifted mom should not force her to embarrass herself singing; explore her likes and dislikes and find what God has given her to use for His glory. No gifts or talents are superior to others. We should not attempt to bend our children's natural skills and talents but enhance and encourage them to blossom fully for God's glory and service.

We should be careful not to confuse charisma with character. Personality is not based on morality and righteousness; it is simply the expression of our God-given uniqueness. Character is the underlying moral base that the child works from, and it must be strong regardless of how he expresses his individuality. Remember it is important to foster and develop the unique personalities and skills with which God has endowed our children; however, our ultimate mission lies in raising young men and women who are full of virtue and godliness.

Quality? Quantity? Both!

At some point in the last twenty years a new and erroneous phrase has popped up in child training. Guilt-ridden parents began saying that it was "quality time" with their children that mattered most. Meaningful exchanges were more important than simply being together. How wrong they were and still are! Meaningful exchanges do not occur when time together has not been spent. Those "Kodak moments" of parent/child relationships do not occur between virtual strangers; they are incidental by-products of hearts woven

> **Quality time does not come without quantity time.**

together during hours spent reading, tickling, running, giggling, cooking, smiling, and talking together.

Tim's Grandpa Max served as father in his young life. Born in 1915 and raised through the Depression, Grandpa Max was a self-reliant, self-made man. He was tough and resourceful, a man of few words. Tim spent many hours at Grandpa's side, mowing lawns, fixing faucets, servicing cars, and counting and cataloging his coin collection. Through Tim's teens and early adulthood, Max remained a silent strength. In his late 80s Grandpa Max grew frail, but Tim's love and respect for his faithful grandfather did not wane. Every other week or so Tim would travel five hours to be with his Gramps. During one such trip, the two of them had been sitting silently for hours, drinking coffee and reading side by side. Grandpa Max lowered his book and with tears misting his eyes said, "I sure am enjoying our conversation, Tim." The irony is that not many words had been spoken. It was time spent together, however quiet, that built the relationship. When Grandpa Max passed away only a few years later, Tim fondly remembered that incident. He realized that looking back over the years, it was not amusement park rides, exotic vacations, white-water rafting or fly-fishing trips that made the most profound impact on his character. It was the casual imparting of wisdom made during hours of tinkering in the garage that made the difference in a young boy's life.

HOW??

Wisdom and character are imparted through *time together!* Deuteronomy 6:6-7 instructs, "And these words, which I command thee this day, shall be in thine heart: and thou shalt teach them *diligently* unto thy children, and shall talk of them *when thou sittest in thine house*, and when thou *walkest by the way*, and when thou *liest down*, and when thou *risest up*." That pretty much covers the day, doesn't it? Rising up. Sitting. Walking. Lying down.

> Success does not compensate for failure at home.

We can already hear your response: "But I'm too busy making a living for my family." "I come home so exhausted at the end of the day." Regardless of time demands and situations that draw you away from home, your family remains a critical priority. When we were in college together, a wise professor gave us a nugget of wisdom. On graduation day he took Tim by the arm and said, "Remember, Tim, success does not compensate for failure at home." The Bible concurs when it asks, "For what shall it profit a man, if he shall gain the whole world and lose his own (or his wife's or his children's) soul?" (Mark 8:36).

> Watch your thoughts; they become words.
> Watch your words; they become actions.
> Watch your actions; they become habits.
> Watch your habits; they become character.
> Watch your character; it becomes your destiny.
> – Frank Outlaw

Remember, it's SIMPLE...

• Wisdom is the second facet of Christian maturity.

• Wisdom is the structure for successful Christian living. Our simple definition of wisdom is "knowledge rightly applied."

• True wisdom takes time and requires growing self-government. It is never too early to begin instilling a love for God, His Word, His ways and people.

• We are to introduce the sweet nectar of God while our newborn children are developing their tastes and appetites, and when they are old, no counterfeit the world might offer them will taste as sweet as what Daddy and Mama have been feeding them since birth.

• Fear not! Instruction in wisdom will not be accomplished in one sitting or even in one year. It is a process. We must look at wisdom as a never-ending lesson; it begins in infancy and ends with our last breaths.

• Read one chapter of the book of Proverbs every day of the month. You will grow in wisdom.

• Do not confuse character with personality. Character denotes moral strength and virtue, whereas personality involves the distinctive qualities, or skills and talents that make each individual unique. We must shape our children's character, while encouraging their personality. Character is the underlying moral base that the child works from, and it must be strong regardless of how he expresses his individuality.

• Meaningful exchanges between parent and child do not occur when time together has not been spent. Quality time does not come without quantity time.

• Wisdom and character are imparted through *time together!*

Chapter Nine
TOOLS OF THE TRADE

*M*odern American culture presents obstacles and pitfalls for the family that were previously unimagined. Divorce. Teenage promiscuity. Hollywood depravity. Latch key kids. Rebellion. Parents have a full-time responsibility to protect their children from "this present darkness." It is important to identify the enemy and be prepared for his overt as well as his more subtle attacks. It is even more vital to be proactive in our training, giving our children a taste for the genuine sweetness of the things of God, and equipping them to live victoriously. In this chapter we will discuss both sides of the issue.

The New Commute

Volumes have been written regarding the radical change in our society brought about by the industrial revolution of the nineteenth century, but its effects on the family are worthy of a brief note. The industrial revolution drastically changed the amount of time families naturally spent together. Prior to machines, factories, and mass production, families worked side by side. Every member of a family was integral in the daily care and keeping of the farm, homestead, or family business. Sons were mentored and apprenticed by their fathers, learning to carry on the family trade. Girls were trained by their mothers in the kitchen, garden, and at the weaving loom, learning her skills along with her wisdom and spirit. What a contrast to our modern society! Today children spend countless hours each day at school only to come home to an empty house while Dad and Mom are both off chasing the dollar, either not understanding or just ignoring the treasures that are home alone.

Home Wrecker

After a decade of marriage and family counseling, we can personally attest to the devastation that divorce brings to the lives of children. Of all marriages today, somewhere between 40 and 60% will end in divorce, a statistic that is surprisingly mirrored in Christian marriages. Every year one million American children see their parents divorce.[15] Studies have shown that these innocent victims suffer life-long repercussions. It is our personal conclusion that much of the degeneration of society in general is due to the prevalence of divorce. Jesus, in Matthew 12:25 warns, "Every kingdom divided against itself is brought to desolation; and every city or house divided against itself shall not stand."

If approximately 50% of all marriages end in divorce, there is a pretty high probability that you or someone close to you has experienced its devastation first hand. We are in no way indicting you. In fact, we ache for you, knowing the pain and disappointment you have experienced. But please don't be disheartened. Psalm

27:10 promises, "When my father and mother forsake me, then the Lord will he take me up." You and Jesus can make all the difference in repairing the damage.

The Box

"On July 26, 2000, the American Health Association, American Academy of Pediatrics, American Psychological Association, American Psychiatric Association, American Academy of Family Physicians, and the American Academy of Child & Adolescent Psychiatry published a *Joint Statement on The Impact of Entertainment Violence on Children* in which they reported sobering research results:

"Viewing entertainment violence can lead to increase in aggressive attitudes, values and behavior, particularly in children. Its effects are measurable and long lasting. Moreover, prolonged viewing of media violence can lead to emotional desensitization toward violence in real life."

"Children who see a lot of violence are more likely to view violence as an effective way of settling conflicts. Children exposed to violence are more likely to assume that acts of violence are acceptable behavior."

"Although less research has been done on the impact of violent interactive entertainment (such as video games) on young people, preliminary studies indicate that the negative impact may be significantly more severe than that wrought by television, movies or music." [16]

Is that a concise enough indictment of television? We have not even mentioned Hollywood's agenda for our families. If you are not convinced of television's detrimental effect on our families and country, you can access at least 22 research reports from reputable agencies such as Harvard School of Public Health, Journal of the

American Medical Association (JAMA), Journal of the American Academy of Child and Adolescent Psychiatry, and Journal of Applied Developmental Psychology at www.lionlamb.org.

The King family's solution is not to own a television. More and more Christians are realizing that there is life after the "tube." Think of the hours of family fun you can have without it!

Kid Culture

CNN reported that in 1997, 45% of teenage boys and 38 % of teenage girls were sexually active, contrasted with 1970, when 5% of 15-year-old girls said they'd experienced sex and 1972 when 20% of 15-year-old boys said they'd had sex.[17] In similarly disturbing studies, the National Institute on Drug Abuse found that in 2002, 36% of 12th graders had smoked marijuana and that 53% of 12th graders had tried some form of illicit drugs.[18] We do not intend to paint a bleak portrait of teen life in America. Unfortunately, troubled teens are the ones who get the most press, so those are the ones of which the public is most aware. On the other hand, there is a growing segment of wonderful, responsible kids out there. We want to encourage you to know who your children are running with. Invite their friends to spend some time with you. Do not assume that because a child has Christian parents, he is a good influence on your children. The Bible warns us in Proverbs 13:20, "He that walketh with wise men shall be wise: but a companion of fools shall be destroyed." You know the old saying, "One bad apple spoils the bunch."

The Stuff of Life

We knew of a successful architect who was building a "dream home" for his big family. Mr. and Mrs. Brown had six children and lived in a 3,000 square foot home, but they felt that they needed more space. Because their new home took longer to build than they expected, they moved temporarily into a 900 square foot bungalow. In order for eight people to fit into such a tiny house, they had to be ruthless about what they moved in and what went into storage. The children found themselves sharing bedrooms for the first time in years.

The Browns were apprehensive about their temporary home. Every member of the family privately expected it to be a rough stay, anticipating that in such close quarters they would quickly get on each other's nerves. Just the opposite occurred. After the first few months, the Brown children realized that they enjoyed each other's company. They talked excitedly about their day at school, laughing together as they crowded around the little dinner table. They began playing games and reading good books aloud together, rather than retreating to their individual bedrooms as they had in their larger home. When Mr. Brown related his experience to a mutual friend, he was so happy with the positive changes in his children that he was undecided as to whether or not he would ever move his family into their spacious new home when it was completed. The Browns were seriously considering staying in the little bungalow that had drawn their scattered family back together!

Materialism is a hypnotic force in our American society. Last year's car model is obsolete. Some wouldn't be caught dead in last spring's fashions. "Wide toed shoes are out, haven't you heard?" "You are going to Hawaii for vacation? How common! The Smiths are going to Bora Bora." We can become so caught up in attaining *things* that we neglect the people we love. The Browns shook off the hypnotic appeal of "stuff" in time and rediscovered that they were related to a bunch of wonderful people!

Sometimes we need to make radical changes for the good of our family.

Think on THESE Things

We must actively pursue the means by which to avoid snares of the prevailing culture. We must act or be acted upon. Do not be deceived; this is not a halfhearted conviction. Much is at stake and the enemy is cunning. "Be sober, be vigilant; because your adversary the devil, as a roaring lion, walketh about, seeking whom he may devour" (1 Peter 5:7). However, when we are "steadfast in the faith" (v. 8), we receive the promise that He will "make [us] perfect, establish, strengthen, settle [us]" (v.10). That is a promise worth fighting for! Remember our goal is successful, mature children who are full of self-control, wisdom, and responsibility.

Our most proactive weapon against the garbage and confusion of this age is to fill our children's ears, eyes, minds, hours, and days with good things. "Finally, brethren, whatsoever things are true, whatsoever things are honest, whatsoever things are just, whatsoever things are pure, whatsoever things are lovely, whatsoever things are of a good report; if there be any virtue, and if there be any praise, think on these things" (Philippians 4:8). Because we want this to be a how-to book with specific suggestions for doing just that, we offer the following ideas for imparting God's all-important wisdom to our children as they grow.

Tool Chest

DEVOTION AND BIBLE TRAINING—Our wise pastor counsels our home church to set one night aside each week for family devotions. There are many great devotional guides that offer serial lessons, character studies, or a potpourri of subjects. There are innumerable ways to study the Bible. Some families choose to study the stories chronologically, while others prefer studying great men and women of the Bible. They use either the Bible itself or good Bible storybooks. Again we will suggest the Book of Proverbs to you. It is not too ambitious to daily read one chapter of Proverbs (or even a few choice verses) aloud to your family. God's Word never returns void.

FAMILY NIGHT—Monday night is family night in the King home. Although extenuating circumstances occasionally preempt our evening, it is an appointment that we all guard against the encroaching busy-ness of life. We begin with a real dinner. There is usually a tablecloth and centerpiece (which could be someone's Pooh-bear, or flowers picked from the garden—the children take turns with their individual creativity). The menu is not typically gourmet, but it is a break from fast food fare. After an unhurried dinner and table talk, we all clean the kitchen together. Our usual KP rule is that "the cook doesn't clean," but things are special on Monday night. We then settle in on the family room couches for whatever Bible reading, study, or lesson Dad has prepared; however, to "keep 'em guessing" we have been known to surprise the children with something out of the ordinary.

We discuss prayer requests and spend some time in prayer, either collectively or individually. We teach our children the Lord's Prayer when they are very young, and how to use it as a structure upon which to praise, thank, pray for our nation and leaders, request, ask forgiveness, guidance, strength, discernment, and wisdom. When the children are young and learning, we keep them next to us and pray loudly enough to direct their own prayers, leading by example. After prayer, we may just talk, do an object lesson to illustrate a truth, play a game, take a walk, or a surprise drive to Vic's, our favorite old-fashioned ice cream shop. In what manner you choose to personalize family night is not the issue; it's the value you place on your family by setting one entire evening aside for them! This is a rich and primary time of imparting God's all-important wisdom.

Keep it simple and do-able.

TABLE TALK—Already mentioned above, table talk is a fulfillment of the Deuteronomy chapter six admonition to teach at all times. We have lamented the dizzying pace of our society, and family dinnertime seems to be a casualty of that plague. Recently a grandmother worried aloud in a small group of women about the fact her grandchildren eat the majority of their meals in the back seat of their SUV, hurrying from one obligation to the next. Her daughter is one of the best mamas we know, and her children are destined for greatness. But this grandmother understands the value of table talk. This is where Daddy and Mama catch up on the events of the day; school happenings, reminders, sibling scuffles, current national and world events, why spiders have so many legs…. We occasionally use the conversation-sparking cards from the old "Un-Game" when we want something different; in the last few years, Franklin-Covey came out with a line of table-talk cards for both families with young children and for teens. They have ignited many insightful discussions in our home.

GOOD OLD LITERATURE AND GODLY STORIES—Fill your library and your time with good literature: *Little Lord Fauntleroy, The Little Princess, Anne of Green Gables, Swiss Family Robinson, Titus*

Companion of the Cross, Little House on the Prairie, Elsie Dinsmore and *Little Britches* series, *Foxes Book of Martyrs* (really!), *The Chronicles of Narnia, Wizard of Oz, Charlotte's Web, Charlie and the Chocolate Factory,* biographies of American and Christian heroes, anything by G.A. Henty, and on and on. There is no sermon on character that can instruct better than a good, godly story. Oh, the discussion that followed a chapter of *Little Lord Fauntleroy*: "Mama, I want to be as kind as Cedric is. He never loses his temper with the bad people." Wow! There is no way for us to convey how the characters of our children have been shaped by the likes of Anne Shirley, Sarah Crewe, Ralph Moody, Templeton the rat, or Augustus Galoop and Mike Teevee.

If there were only two storybooks we could recommend to you, they would be *The King's Daughter* and *Tiger and Tom*. These 170-year-old reprinted books are timeless classics of character and morals. They are compilations of brief stories that portray children attempting to act and think with courage, integrity, and Christian character. They encourage boys to become men and girls to become true ladies, not just women! You will find the language pure and uplifting, void of the watering down that is prevalent today. Each story is brief enough to read before nap or bedtime or even at the dinner table. We often encourage the children to finish their duties quickly so that we will have time for "a *Tiger and Tom*." Do not miss this investment in eternity.

BIBLE ON CD/PREACHING TAPES—We purchased the complete Bible on compact disk a few years ago and have not been sorry. The Bible promises that when God's Word issues forth, it will not return void but will produce fruit. "So shall my word be that goeth forth out of my mouth: it shall not return unto me void, but it shall accomplish that which I please and it shall prosper in the thing whereto I send it" (Isaiah 55:11). We claim these promises and often set a CD player in a place where all of the children can hear the soothing Word of God as they drift off to sleep. We know of many four- or five-year-olds that can quote lengthy portions of their favorite sermon tapes. Whether in the car or at naptime, simply letting the words of ageless wisdom resound in our homes changes the atmosphere from harried and chaotic to tranquil and peaceful. Remember, "…and shall talk of them *when thou sittest in thine house*, and when thou *walkest by the way*, and when thou *liest down*, and when thou *risest up*."

GODLY STORIES DRAMATIZED—This is a super combination of the last two suggestions. There are a few outstanding productions of character and Bible stories dramatized. "Your Story Hour" is our family favorite. They have sets of cassette tapes that dramatize the major events, persons, and stories of the Bible. They are comprehensive and compelling. They also offer dramatizations of great characters in human history: men and women who have surmounted odds and done extraordinary things, such as Orville and Wilbur Wright, Henry Ford, Glen Cunningham, Marie Curie, Clara Barton, Booker T. Washington, and many more worthy heroes of history and faith. They also have moral and character stories, usually involving children faced with common moral decisions or temptations and how they overcome them. These stories evoke the refreshing feeling of moral purity of a bygone era.

New resources have appeared in the last few years that are also powerful tools. Focus on the Family Radio Theater has done an outstanding job of dramatizing such Christian classics as *Les Miserable*, the entire *Chronicles of Narnia series*, *A Christmas Carol*, *Ben Hur*, *The Secret*

Garden, The Legend of Squanto, Billy Bud, Sailor, and many others. They have carefully maintained the authors' intended Christian moral.

Note: We do not intend to turn this section into a product review; however, we want to make you aware of the tools that have proven fruitful for our family and many others.

OBJECT LESSONS—This is Kirsten's favorite way to break complex principles of life and truth into bite size pieces for little ones. Object lessons are powerful tools that are appropriate for children of all ages. This was driven home when we spent two years assisting in an inner-city outreach church. Many of the adults had limited exposure to or understanding of biblical wisdom. Each week Tim would bring a simple object lesson to the entire congregation. Years later, adults still comment on how those illustrations helped them in their early walk with God.

So what do you do? Allow us to give you one fun example:

We wanted to illustrate the Bible as our guide to navigating through life. We chose Psalm 119:105, "Thy word is a lamp unto my feet, and a light unto my path," to demonstrate. On family night, after dinner cleanup, we shooed all of the children into the boys' bedroom with explicit instructions not to come out until we came for them. We quickly rearranged the living room furniture, moving the couch and love seat into the middle of the room, and stacking their cushions and toss pillows in random piles throughout the room. Tim hung a sheet from the ceiling across the hallway entrance, and we turned off all the lights, making the entire area pitch black. We were ready for the lesson. We brought our oldest child, Adam, out first. Kirsten guided him down the darkened hallway. As some foreign object (the sheet) brushed his forehead, Adam ducked and flailed his arms in alarm. Carefully, Mama led the boy into the first stumbling block—a pillow tower.

Bump! "Whoa, what was that?"

"It's okay son. Just do your best…feel your way."

"Ouch! Who moved the coffee table?" He exclaimed as he knocked his leg into an obstacle, "Mom, I can't see anything. Help me out here."

Finally Adam made it across the room with no major mishaps. Now Dad turned on the flashlight he held in his hand.

"Let's try it again, Son. This time we'll use this little light." We began again at the mysterious floating object.

"Oh, it's just a sheet! That freaked me out! I didn't know what it was."

Slowly, with the aid of one small flashlight, Adam navigated the obstacle course that was our darkened living room. As he did, his dad offered the application.

"You see, Son, God's Word is like this little flashlight. It lights your path, exposing all of the dangers and pitfalls in this otherwise dark world. Without the Word, we are simply stumbling blindly in the dark."

"Wow. That was fun…can I do it again?"

"I tell you what, you sit here quietly and listen. I'm going to go get Emily now. Don't give it away!" A few minutes later a stifled giggle was heard from the vicinity of the dangling UFO in the hallway. That night's lesson is one the Kings still laugh about. We all have a living picture to illustrate the importance of looking to the Word of God for direction in life.

There are hundreds of object lesson books geared to children of all ages. Most require little or no money, and minimal preparation. The time invested yields great dividends.

MOTTOS, SAYINGS, AND REMINDERS—

You may have noticed that we are drawn to catchy little sayings that encapsulate bigger thoughts. We have found that mottos, jingles, or sayings that are easily remembered, are very effective ways to leave indelible reminders. Think about it: "Just Do It" (Nike), "You deserve a break today" (McDonalds), "Have it your way" (Burger King). These companies paid someone millions of dollars to create their jingles and slogans, understanding their power of influence on us. We have sprinkled some of our mottos and sayings among the powerful quotes from others in sidebar boxes so that you may either use them or be inspired to create your own. They work; ask Ronald McDonald!

Overwhelmed?

Don't be! Remember, training in biblical truths, wisdom, and character is incremental; it is not a quick fix, but a lifetime investment. We did not implement all of these tools at once, neither would we expect you to. In fact, we would say *don't*. Pick one thing to concentrate on, preferably weekly family night and devotions. Start small. Have success. When many parents hear the word *devotions*, their first feeling is *guilt*. They have lofty plans to wake their children at six a.m. for daily, comprehensive doctrine training and electrifying prayer meeting. When the plans fold on the third day, they feel like failures. Someone wisely said that success breeds success. Please re-read our caution to set wimpy goals at the end of chapter five. Your small accomplishments will build up momentum and propel your family to desire more successes. You will be actively fulfilling the directive of Deuteronomy 6:7-8, by training up your children in a very important facet of Christian maturity.

Remember, it's SIMPLE...

• It is important to identify the enemy and be prepared for his overt as well as his more subtle attacks.

• It is even more vital to be proactive in our training, giving our children a taste for the genuine sweetness of the things of God, and equipping them to live victoriously.

• The New Commute - Every member of a family was integral in the daily care and keeping of the farm, homestead, or family business. Today children spend countless hours each day at school only to come home to an empty house while Dad and Mom are both off chasing the dollar, either not understanding or just ignoring the treasures that are home alone.

• Home Wrecker - Of all marriages today, approximately 50% will end in divorce. Every year one million American children see their parents divorce. [15] Studies have shown that these innocent victims suffer life-long repercussions.

• The Box - The television has brought a new level of violence and degradation to our society. Statistics are increasingly finding it's detrimental effect on children.

• Kid Culture - Drug abuse and sexual promiscuity are continuing to be a plague among American teens.

• We must actively pursue the means by which to avoid snares of the prevailing culture. We must act or be acted upon. Do not be deceived; this is not a halfhearted conviction. Much is at stake and the enemy is cunning.

Our Tool Chest

Devotion and Bible Training- There are many great devotional guides that offer serial lessons, character studies, or a potpourri of subjects

Family Night - In what manner you choose to personalize family night is not the issue; it's the value you place on your family by setting one entire evening aside for them!

Table Talk - Table talk is a fulfillment of the Deuteronomy six admonition to teach at all times.

Good Old Literature and Godly Stories- There is no sermon on character that can instruct better than a good, godly story.

Bible on CD/Preaching Tapes- The Bible promises that when God's Word issues forth, it will not return void but will produce fruit.

Godly Stories Dramatized- These make Bible and moral stories come to life for the young listener.

Object Lessons- Object lessons are powerful tools that are appropriate for children of all ages.

Mottos, Sayings, and Reminders- We have found that mottos, jingles, or sayings that are easily remembered, are very effective ways to leave indelible reminders.

• Remember, training in biblical truths, wisdom, and character is incremental; it is not a quick fix, but a lifetime investment.

• Begin slowly and build on success!

Chapter Ten

WISDOM OF
THE AGES

When Corrie ten Boom, holocaust heroine and author of The Hiding Place, was five years old she accompanied her father on a business trip to Amsterdam. Her father had purchased a number of parts for his watch-making business; the parts were packed in a large suitcase.

As the train neared their home station, Corrie asked her dad, "What is sex sin?"

After carefully weighing his thoughts, he said to her, "Corrie, please carry the suitcase for me." She struggled to obey but could not lift the heavy valise. "Papa, it is too heavy for me to carry."

Papa responded, "Yes, Corrie, and so is the answer to your question. So, until you are old enough to carry the answer, I will carry it for you."

Like the wise Mr. ten Boom, we will have to discern which questions and situations are "too heavy" for our children. We must be cautious not to load down our children with the bleak baggage of this world before they are able to carry it. It takes a wise parent to weigh out the balance between maintaining our children's innocence and equipping them with the godly wisdom necessary to make sound choices and decisions. It would be disastrous to approach the two-year-old with the same level of expectations as we would the seven-year-old.

There are myriad opportunities and methods for instructing our children in godly wisdom. In order to do it most effectively, it is important to note the stages of understanding and moral need. This is a good place to look at the stages of moral understanding our children pass through. Knowing these stages will enable us to better apply the methods of wisdom training we introduced in the previous chapter. Please do not take this list as a comprehensive, fixed scope and sequence of cognitive development. The ages associated with each stage are simply rough estimates. Just as with walking and talking, all children develop morally and spiritually at their own pace!

Sustenance, Structure, and Conditioning

AGES 0–18 MONTHS

The physical and cognitive development that occurs in the first 24 months of life is nothing short of miraculous. We stand amazed as our little cherubs triple or quadruple in weight, double in height, go from immobile little bundles of complete helplessness to running, talking, laughing, singing, kissing, hugging, ball-throwing and chair-climbing human beings! Although the primary parental responsibility during these developmental wonder months are food, clothing, shelter, protection, guidance, and love, many parents do not realize that it is time to begin self-control and wisdom training. It is never too early to let your little ones hear the soothing Word of God, listen to Daddy tell stories of Jonah and David, or learn songs about Jesus. Love and nurture your little treasures, being careful not to develop habits that strengthen their self-will.

Foundation of Obedience

AGES 18 MONTHS TO 8 YEARS

The section on self-control in this book, chapters 3-7, is geared to this group of kids. During these years the focus on self-control and attitude is primary, and the job is 24/7/365. We spend the bulk of our time bringing our children's wills under subjection to the standards and rules that we have set. During this time we are also laying a spiritual and moral foundation for our children. Children learn to pray with Daddy and Mama, sing to Jesus, worship and respond properly in church, listen to Bible and moral stories, and memorize Scriptures. Parents lead devotions and introduce good character traits. All of these building blocks are set in the growing base of moral training at this stage.

Moral and Character Training

AGES 8 TO 12

By eight years old, the intense focus on self-control, attitude, and obedience training should be tapering off. We still require instant obedience and cheerful, respectful attitudes; however, if self-control, attitude, and obedience training has been administered early and consistently, there should be few, if any, incidents that require chastisement after 10 years of age. Although we are tempted to kick back and wipe our brow in relief that our little cherubs have survived the action-packed toddler and primary years, we must not rest on our laurels. These years are prime time for fine-tuning the character and spirit of our children. This is a time of emotional and physical transition from childhood to adulthood via the oft-feared teen years. Our job is now likened to teaching our children to ride a bicycle: After careful instruction, we give them a good running start and let go. We jog alongside our unsure, wobbly-wheeled beginners, ready to right them if they start to weave too far out of control. We call out instruction and encouragement as they conquer this monumental step of independence. As we did with the bike rider, we run alongside as our child tries out his growing independence. We are close enough to give little instructions and corrections or even to catch him, should there be an unforeseen speed bump or barking dog. We are gradually letting go.

These years are prime time for fine-tuning the character and spirit of our children.

At this age the parent/child relationship moves to a more mature level. The right to respectfully appeal and understand the "why" of a directive comes into play when the child has demonstrated cheerful compliance. Your relationship is changing from the monarchy of early childhood ("I, your parent, reign supreme. I say it, you do it, period!"), to a republic ("You may respectfully present your position for discussion and consideration, Son, but I still hold *veto* power!"). For example, your child is outside playing basketball with a neighbor. You call to him to come inside to clean up and set the table for dinner.

He stops playing and respectfully says, "Yes, Mom. We are playing 21, and I'm at 19. May I finish and then come in for my chores?"

This is a reasonable request asked with a good attitude. He does not whine or continue playing and ignore you. From his attitude and response you can tell that he will cheerfully obey if your answer to his appeal is no; however, his request is reasonable and you honor his right response with, "Sure Son. Come in as soon as you whip him" (smile).

Your willingness to concede to your children's appeals depends on their willingness to obey cheerfully if their appeals are denied. It all hinges on their attitude. Remember the objective is to train our children to be respectful, responsible adults, and the ability to appeal is a real-life skill. When we give them the right to respectfully appeal we show them honor and respect; we tie those all-important chords of love.

Now is the time to apply the accumulation of Bible and character stories to the child's world. We look for opportunities to point out Bible truths and consequences in everyday life.

"Dad! Mr. Daly paid me $20 for working in his yard this week!" exclaims your excited 11-year-old son.

" Michael, that is wonderful. Mr. Daly called to tell me how impressed he was with your work. He said that you worked hard and with initiative. You didn't have to be told about each little job and did more than what you were asked. He wants to know if you can help him clean out his garage this Saturday. Do you see why he asked you to come back?"

"I worked hard and fast, Dad."

"I am proud of you, Son. God's Word is right. The hand of the diligent makes a man rich, but lazy hands make us poor. Good job, Mike."

Building relationship in these years is vital. Be a friend. Listen. The bridges that you build now will become vital passes over the potentially turbulent emotional waters of the coming teen years. Remember the goal of parenting is to train up our children to be self-controlled, wise, responsible, and mature adults. We see each stage of their young lives as opportunities to layer instruction to that end.

Consulting and Coaching

AGES 13–20

If parenting our children through the middle years is illustrated by teaching them to ride a two-wheeler, then the teen years could be compared to coaching a tackle football team. You, the coach, practice with your players throughout the season. You lead them in calisthenics and running long distances, building endurance and flexibility. You have planning meetings, exposing the strategy of the opposition and preparing your own successful game plan. You oversee the team as they practice plays time after time, until the right moves seem to become automatic responses. You foster team spirit and bolster morale. After countless hours of practice on the home field, you stand on the sidelines as you watch your team enter the game of life. Now you must pace outside the play of the game, watching, praying, and hoping that they will correctly execute all of those well-laid plans. Occasionally you enter the field for a time-out to remind the players of the game plan, hear their concerns, and encourage them to victory.

We coach and guide our children in these years in such areas as finding the will of God for their profession, using their talents in the Kingdom of God in some facet of ministry, and planning and attending higher education to prepare themselves for their vocation and calling. We guide them through the sometimes-choppy waters of male/female relationships, advising caution in the realm of dating and courtship, and helping them to remain levelheaded in the midst of topsy-turvy hormones and emotions. We lead and train them in being responsible with their finances: getting their first job, giving, saving, and spending wisely, opening bank accounts, purchasing first cars and insurance, understanding the pros and cons of credit and credit cards, making practical financial goals, and eventually moving into their own home, etc. Years of strengthening those silken cords of love around our children have forged a relationship built on love and respect. Our adult children ask for our guidance and listen to our wisdom.

We recently spoke to an older mother who is a great candidate for "coach of the year." Her three grown sons are testimonies to their parents' wisdom. They all are successful, and they have lovely, Christian wives and happy, energetic children. She let us peek in on one of her secrets of success when she related the following story. One of her sons, we will call him Jeff, was engaged to marry a young woman who his mother and father were realizing was not who she had initially appeared to be. Late one night Jeff came to his parents' bedroom; it was obvious that the young man was troubled.

"Dad, Mom, what do you think of Gina?"

"She is a nice girl, Son."

"Yes, she's nice. But I am asking what you really think," Jeff pressed.

"Well, Son," began his hesitant mother. "I've been noticing some things that I'm not sure I had noticed before...."

Not commanding, but leading him to his own conclusions, Jeff's wise parents were able to point out some valid concerns to their son. Our goal with our teenagers is independent wisdom, so we work toward that mark by letting them talk through their harder decisions and feelings with us and by guiding them through the maze. The days of "my way or the highway" are passed. We have nurtured, bent, trained, preached, cried, cajoled, and led. Now is the time that we increasingly let them make decisions, and their decisions reveal to us how much of what we have taught and modeled is in their hearts and understanding. These are the years of reward for all of our hard work. Our children will be pleasant company. They will bring honor to their parents.

Grossed Out or Grieved

How do you and your children react when you see a young man with a purple Mohawk and multiple rings through his face? Do you mock his girlfriend with the flaming skull tattoo and the skimpy clothing? It has been important to us to teach our children not to be "grossed out" by the sin and depravity we see. When we see the wayward, young couple or the drunkard stumbling down the street, we grieve with compassion, not judgment, at the toll that alcohol and drugs take on the body, and discuss the trap that these sinful habits create.

> Children have more need of models, than of critics.
> – Joseph Joubert

"Oh, how sad. Those young people are really trying to find something to fill the void in their lives, aren't they? They look so tough on the outside, but their hearts are empty and sad."

"Don't stare at the man, Sweetie. He is different, but we want to see him as Jesus does. Do you remember King Solomon's warnings about the seductive wooing of sin? It looks good and feels good at first, but before you know it you are hooked, and it ruins your life. 'The wages of sin is death.'"

Mocking and criticizing people for their lifestyle or looks lead to a loss of basic human respect. Show your child by your example of grief over the disabled, the different, or "down-and-out," and, instead of cynicism, they will learn love and compassion.

Warning: Do not lie about the pleasures of sin!

When our children are young we tell them that sex, drugs, and alcohol are bad. We warn them not to touch. We are right—drugs, alcohol, tobacco, and promiscuity ruin countless lives. We must avoid them, period. However, people drink and get high because they like the "good" feeling. It is pleasurable. The fact that we explain this honestly when our children grow older may alarm some parents, but remember that God is honest with us when He says, "for a season, sin is pleasurable" (Hebrews 11:25). We feel that it is important to warn our maturing children that sin may not necessarily *feel* bad, but that God's Word emphatically promises a ruined life and eventual death for those who sin. If you simply say that those things (drugs, alcohol, promiscuity, etc.) are gross, and your child falls, even once, and enjoys a "sampling" of sin, he may wonder what else you have lied about!

Warning: Do not lie about the pleasures of sin!

The same warning holds for the pleasures of sexuality. God made everything good, and when He made woman for man He said it was very good. The sexual relationship between a husband and wife is one of those "very good" benefits. Sex outside of the covenant of marriage is the wrong thing at the wrong time. In over ten years of pre-marital counseling we have repeatedly seen young women whose attitudes toward marital intimacy are skewed by what they had been told all through their childhood: "Sex is bad." Yes, sex is wrong before marriage; pre-marital promiscuity and fornication are epidemic in our society. The result is too many single-parent homes. However, sex itself is not bad. Sex is intended to be a pleasurable union between committed marriage partners, designed to cement and draw closer two loving partners. It is beautiful within the God-ordained covenant of marriage. When physical intimacy precedes that covenant, it is wrong and brings harm and destruction to the participants. When following God's order of events—waiting in abstinence for the perfect mate, then being joined in marriage—sex is a wholesome, pleasurable thing.

The Apostle John said, "I have no greater joy than to hear that my children walk in truth" (3 John 4). This is the testimony we coveted when as young parents we watched beautiful families serving God and enjoying one another. This is the testimony of the parents who lead and guide their children in the ways of self-control and godly wisdom. Now let's round out our definition of Christian maturity by looking at the third facet: responsibility, in the next section.

Remember, it's SIMPLE...

There are myriad opportunities and methods for instructing our children in godly wisdom. In order to do it most effectively, it is important to note the stages of understanding and moral need.

SUSTENANCE, STRUCTURE, & CONDITIONING
AGES 0–18 MONTHS

- During this stage, children triple or quadruple in weight, double in height, go from immobile little bundles of complete helplessness to running, talking, laughing, singing, kissing, hugging, ball-throwing and chair-climbing human beings!

- Although the primary parental responsibility during these developmental wonder months are food, clothing, shelter, protection, guidance, and love, many parents do not realize that it is time to begin self-control and wisdom training.

FOUNDATION OF OBEDIENCE
AGES 18 MONTHS TO 8 YEARS

- During these years the focus on self-control and attitude is primary.

- We spend the bulk of our time bringing our children's wills under subjection to the standards and rules that we have set.

- We are also laying a spiritual and moral foundation for our children.

MORAL AND CHARACTER TRAINING
AGES 8 TO 12 YEARS

- These years are prime time for fine-tuning the character and spirit of our children.

- By eight years old, the intense focus on self-control, attitude, and obedience training should be tapering off.

- At this age the parent/child relationship moves to a more mature level.

•We look for opportunities to point out Bible truths and consequences in everyday life.

•Building relationship in these years is vital. Be a friend. Listen.

CONSULTING AND COACHING
AGES 13–20 YEARS

• Like the football coach, we practice, instruct, coach and then stand on the sidelines watching to see how our child executes all of the well practiced plans.

• Our adult children ask for our guidance and listen to our wisdom.

• It has been important to us to teach our children not to be "grossed out" by the sin and depravity we see. Mocking and criticizing people for their lifestyle or looks lead to a loss of basic human respect. Show your child by your example of grief over the disabled, the different, or "down-and-out," and, instead of cynicism, they will learn love and compassion.

• **Warning: Do not lie about the pleasures of sin!** It is important to warn our maturing children that sin may not necessarily *feel* bad, but that God's Word emphatically promises a ruined life and eventual death for those who sin.

PART THREE

HELPING YOUR CHILD
Become...

RESPONSIBLE

Chapter Eleven

FACE THE MUSIC

*E*arlier in the book we spent a great deal of time on the virtue of self-control. Again, we must emphasize that self-control is absolutely foundational to success in the lives of our children. Self-control is essential to spiritual victory as well as to accomplishments or success in the natural world, whether emotional, relational, or material. Children who will reach incredible heights are those who can restrain their passions and appetites, resist the many "trees of temptation," and do what they know they should do rather than what they want to do. Their potential is limitless! However, to expect responsible actions from self-indulgent, unbridled children is like the foolish builder in Matthew seven who expected his house on the sand to stand firm. Although the house looked sturdy, when torrential storms pounded relentlessly, the house fell. The base was faulty; the foundation was built on error. The Scripture accentuated the ruin by stating, "...and great was the fall of it" (Matthew 7:27). Children who cannot control their cravings will become adults who cannot control their cravings. In fact, these desires can become all consuming and ruinous, for the flesh is never satisfied.

Sadly, we see irresponsibility and the havoc it wreaks all around us in our increasingly unrestrained society. Violent and corporate crime, divorce, bankruptcy, parents abandoning their children, adult children neglecting and abusing their own parents, and many other dismal signs and disheartening statistics are on the rise. We see personal responsibility fade as a priority in our country and culture. Most of us long to interact with individuals of integrity. As children of the Wise King, we are responsible to stand against the tide of hedonism and operate with integrity, honor, reliability, honesty, and virtue befitting the "royal priesthood." Character that is truly responsible is character set apart. Charisma, which can be temporarily mistaken for character, can take people only so far in life, however grit and fortitude, which truly virtuous and upright individuals display, set them apart as people of excellence. Because such individuals are becoming fewer and farther between in this society of self-gratification and excess, their characters shine among the ordinary, and they are often elevated to positions of leadership and respect. Should we be surprised when this happens? No. Scripture tells us, "Seest thou a man diligent in his business? He shall stand before kings; he shall not stand before mean men" (Proverbs 22:29). Also, "the diligent maketh rich" (Proverbs 10:4), and "the hand of the diligent shall bear rule" (Prov. 12:24). We, as Christian parents, want to see our children rise up and become dependable, productive, contributing leaders of society.

Before proceeding farther into the third facet of Christian maturity—responsibility—take a moment and reflect on your family. Have you begun making self-control a parenting priority? Are you consciously and deliberately working on developing self-restraint in your children in the ways we have suggested? Are you reaping the peaceable fruit of righteousness?

Are they learning to bridle their impulses? Do you see growing maturity and self-discipline? No, we are not asking if they are perfect little cherubs

> They cannot take away our self respect unless we give it to them.
> – Mahatma Gandhi

yet! Who of us are? We are suggesting that you "take inventory" because we do not want you to begin teaching responsibility if you are not yet diligent in matters of "flesh" control. Responsibility is truly an outgrowth of self-control. Although we cannot delay training in responsibility until our young ones demonstrate faultless self-control, we must not neglect one while we focus on the other. Children should grow in all three facets of Christian maturity—self-control, wisdom, and responsibility—simultaneously and incrementally.

Responsibility

A concise, working definition of responsibility is twofold: "accepting personal accountability for one's own actions," and "faithful and conscientious work habits." [19] The first component of responsibility we want our children to possess is personal accountability. Steven Covey, in his best-selling personal leadership book, *The Seven Habits of Highly Effective People*, points out that the definition of responsibility lies in the composition of the word itself—response-ability—the ability to choose one's response. "Highly proactive people recognize that responsibility. They do not blame circumstances, conditions, or conditioning for their behavior. Their behavior is a product of their own conscious choice, based on values, rather than a product of their conditions, based on feelings." [20] Read that definition again! Think about it. We want to purposefully raise children who are self-controlled enough to act virtuously regardless of the circumstance (rather than react to their influences) and then accept responsibility for their actions, both good and bad. Their salvation hinges on it!

In our carnal state we look for ways to escape liability for misconduct, denying that we have sinned. Denying our sinful acts and nature will lead to eternal damnation. As Christians, we know that "if we confess our sins, he is faithful and just to forgive us our sins, and to cleanse us from all unrighteousness" (1 John 1:9). If we do not accept blame for our wrongdoings, we will not confess them and be cleansed. This vital lesson is contrary to our very nature. The temptation from the dawn of time has been to shirk responsibility and blame our wrongdoing on someone or something else: bad timing, wrong information, sickness, hunger, fatigue, or other creative excuses and rationales ad infinitum. We jokingly say that the second sin in the Bible was shifting blame. Adam told God that he ate the forbidden fruit because of Eve. Eve blamed her fall to temptation on the smooth-talking salesmanship of the serpent, "But, God, it's not my fault...I have a good explanation."

> **No one can hurt you without your consent.**
> – Eleanor Roosevelt

"Hast thou eaten of the tree, whereof I commanded thee that thou shouldest not eat?" God asked Adam what he had done.

Adam answered with history's first excuse: "The woman, whom thou gavest to be with me, she gave me of the tree, and I did eat." Did you hear Adam almost blaming God for his own disobedience? "Well, *you* gave me that woman, and *she* made me do it." Deny. Blame. Excuse.

The Lord then turned to Eve: "What is it that thou hast done?"

"The serpent beguiled me, and I did eat."

And so it was the first recorded account of passing the buck!

What? —Not Why?

It is interesting and instructive to note the Lord's line of questioning with the guilty couple above. God did not ask Adam and Eve *why* they had disobeyed and overstepped the divine boundary. He asked them *what* they had done. He was giving them opportunity for confession. When we ask our children *what* deeds they committed, we give them opportunity for confession and cleansing. When we unwisely ask our children *why* they misbehaved, we give them occasion or even encourage them to excuse, explain away, or even lie about their behavior. There is never an excuse for evildoing. Excuses will not help children mature in taking responsibility but will stunt their growth! Children can become cunning at the arts of manipulation and excuse making.

Consider the following scenario: Logan and Elise are playing quietly in Logan's bedroom when a bloodcurdling, female scream pierces the calm. Mom rushes to the scene to find that Logan has obviously given his best karate chop to his sister's cheek.

"*What* happened here, Son?" Mother asks over the sobs of the offended daughter, cradling her comfortingly.

"She took my best guy," Logan replies defensively, trying to foist some of the guilt onto his sister.

"*What* did *you* do?" Mother persists.

"She was going to break him," he rationalizes.

"What did you do, Son?"

"But she was making a face at me, so I hit her," he defends.

"Is hitting acceptable behavior, Son?"

"She never gets in trouble. It's always me!" Logan attempts to emotionally manipulate his mother by implying favoritism to make her feel guilty.

"We are not talking about Elise right now. We are talking about *what* Logan did. What do you have to say for yourself, Son? Is hitting acceptable behavior?"

Logan dissolves into tears and crumples on the floor, "I'm just so tired, Mom. I don't feel good."

Minutes have passed and Mother approaches the end of her patience. Elise is beginning to calm down but will have a sizeable goose egg from her brother's fit. Logan has yet to assume responsibility for his behavior. He does not feel remorse for hitting his sister. True, he may cry when he is chastised for it, but he cries over his correction not his sin. How can he feel remorse when he feels he has a justifiable reason for violating the family's standards? Do you see the danger in letting such moral relativism go unchecked?

> How much more grievous are the consequences of anger than the causes of it.
> – Marcus Aurelius

The Matthew Seven Principle

Matthew chapter seven contains a core passage relating to personal accountability. It is the ultimate Scripture on confessing and accepting responsibility for our own actions, rather than justifying self and blaming others:

1 Judge not, that ye be not judged.

2 For with what judgment ye judge, ye shall be judged:

and with what measure ye mete, it shall be measured to you again.

3 And why beholdest thou the mote that is in thy brother's eye, but considerest not the beam that is in thine own eye?

4 Or how wilt thou say to thy brother, Let me pull out the mote out of thine eye; and, behold a beam is in thine own eye?

5 Thou hypocrite, first cast out the beam out of thine own eye; and then shall thou see clearly to cast out the mote (literally twig or straw) out of thy brother's eye.

Whether we are counseling married couples, advising friends in business conflict, or negotiating our children through a scuffle, this Scripture is foundational to taking responsibility for our own actions. The actions, attitudes, and even downright dirty offenses of other people are not our concern. We are in no way answerable for the actions of other humans. Their actions may be provocative, sneaky, unfair, mean, or crooked. However, we cannot and will not be able to change anything concerning them. Although the stimulus (the wrong done to us that we would use to justify our wrongdoing) may be enraging, we are accountable for our response to the stimulus. Steven Covey says that the power of greatness lies in the gap between stimulus and response. "It's not what happens to us, but our [wrong] response to what happens to us that hurts us. Of course, things can hurt us physically, or economically and can cause sorrow. But our character, our basic identity, does not have to be hurt at all. In fact, our most difficult experiences become the crucibles that forge our character and develop the internal power, the freedom to handle difficult circumstances in the future and inspire others to do so as well."[20] Responding correctly sets us apart. We must deal with the "beam" in our own eyes, meaning our own faults, weaknesses, and actions.

What inner strength and self-control it takes for a child (or adult) to say simply, "Yes, I did hit my sister"! Character and self-restraint lie in refraining from following the confession with, "It's not fair! She grabbed the guy I was playing with." Or, "She made a face at me." Or, "She said she was going to break my G.I. Joe." Elise's actions do not concern Logan. He is not responsible for his sister's wrong behaviors. He must be confident that Mommy will take care of Sister. Logan's only acceptable response is a contrite, "Yes, I did hit my sister, and I am so sorry." The child who makes that confession without excuse is growing in self-control, wisdom, and favor with the Lord and man! He will surely become a man of greatness. We must work to this end.

> He who angers you conquers you.
> – Elizabeth Kenny

Responsibility in Action:

Model accountability at every opportunity.
Apologize and ask forgiveness when you wrong your spouse or children.

———

Do not defend or make excuses for your child's bad behavior to his teachers, to the ushers at church, or to any adult. Have him accept responsibility for his actions, apologize, and make retribution.

———

If your children break something, have them fix it, replace it, or work off its replacement value if they are too young to have the funds.

—————⇒»•«⇐—————

If your children are grounded or restricted, do not bend the rules if something fun comes along. Let them experience the consequences of their actions.
Do not bail them out!

—————⇒»•«⇐—————

If your children have an engagement or commitment to an activity, do not let them cancel if a more attractive opportunity comes along.

—————⇒»•«⇐—————

If your children leave a mess, have them come back and clean it up.

—————⇒»•«⇐—————

If they leave a light on, they are responsible to turn it off; if they open a door, they are responsible to close it.

—————⇒»•«⇐—————

Hold them to the motto:
DUTY BEFORE PLEASURE
Do what you *must* do first; then enjoy what you *want* to do!

Remember, it's SIMPLE...

- The third facet of Christian maturity is responsibility.

- Self-control is essential to spiritual victory as well as to accomplishments or success in the natural world, whether emotional, relational, or material.

- A character that is truly responsible is a character set apart. Because such individuals are becoming fewer and farther between in this society of self-gratification and excess, their characters shine among the ordinary, and they are often elevated to positions of leadership and respect.

- Responsibility is truly an outgrowth of self-control. Although we cannot delay training in responsibility until our young ones demonstrate faultless self-control, we must not neglect one while we focus on the other. Children should grow in all three facets of Christian maturity—self-control, wisdom, and responsibility—simultaneously and incrementally.

- Responsibility's definition is twofold: "accepting personal accountability for one's own actions," and "faithful and conscientious work habits." [19]

- The temptation from the dawn of time has been to shirk responsibility and blame our wrongdoing on someone or something else: bad timing, wrong information, sickness, hunger, fatigue, or other creative excuses and rationales ad infinitum.

- When we ask our children what deeds they committed, we give them opportunity for confession and cleansing. When we unwisely ask our children why they misbehaved, we give them occasion to excuse, explain away, or even lie about their behavior. There is never an excuse for evildoing.

• Matthew chapter seven contains a core passage relating to personal accountability. It is the ultimate Scripture on confessing and accepting responsibility for our own actions, rather than justifying self and blaming others.

• The child who makes that confession without excuse is growing in self-control, wisdom, and favor with the Lord and man! He will surely become a man of greatness. We must work to this end.

Chapter Twelve
WHISTLE WHILE YOU WORK

*L*ittle Cindy's chubby hands struggled to straighten the top sheet, tugging at one corner and then the other. When the sheet was smoothed to her satisfaction, her attention shifted to the coverlet that her mother had quilted from scraps that had accumulated through the years. Oh, how proud Mommy would be when she saw that her "big girl" had made her own bed! With the last teddy bear situated, she excitedly called to her mother: "I have a surprise for you, Mommy. Come and see, come and see!"

"Oh, Honey, what have you done?"

"I made my bed like a big girl. Aren't you surprised?" The little homemaker could see hesitation on her mother's face as she surveyed the lumpy, disheveled bed.

"Honey, your job is to play. It's Mommy's job to clean and work. Now, run outside, Sweetheart."

Her face drained of its delighted pride and her head hung in disappointment, Cindy trudged solemnly out to the backyard to look for amusement.

Let's fast-forward little Cindy's life 25 years. Her alarm goes off at 5:30 a.m. She must roll out of bed, shower and groom herself, choose and iron her clothes, prepare a healthy breakfast, pack a lunch for later in the day, take something out of the freezer to thaw for dinner, gather all the materials she needs for the 10 a.m. meeting, cheerfully wake the kids, feed, groom and clothe them (including the grumpy, slow-starting, late riser) check to see that everyone's backpack contains last night's homework and the permission slip for the class field trip, feed the cat, herd the crew into the minivan, get gas, kiss the cherubs goodbye at the schoolhouse steps, fight traffic, find the coveted parking spot, arrive at the office ready to face the expectations of a demanding supervisor and greet clients with warmth and calm...all before nine o'clock in the morning! Although Cindy's adult life is a far cry from her responsibility-free childhood, it is not an exaggeration of adult life. Whether our children become doctors, lawyers, teachers, business executives or homemakers (a.k.a. domestic engineers), this is the reality that awaits each boy and girl. The details will vary slightly, but not the frenzied pace, the conflicting demands, or the desperate need for resolve to place duty before pleasure!

Reality Check

An overwhelmed young mom once confided to Kirsten that she felt cheated by her mother's attempts to shield her daughter from the "drudgery" of housework and daily chores. Like little Cindy, she was encouraged to run and play her childhood and young adulthood away. She married young and had three children in rapid succession. She was abruptly faced with running her own household, which completely overwhelmed her. It took more than ten years for this woman to acquire all of the skills necessary for her occupation, and there remains a residual struggle today. Unfortunately, the internal frustration, not to mention that of her extremely patient husband and children, could have been prevented. Many of the lessons she had to learn the hard way in adulthood, she could have learned at her mother's side as a growing girl.

Remember our goal as Christian parents is to prepare our children as they develop to maturity and readiness for adult responsibilities. The second facet of responsibility is faithful and conscientious work habits. A large chunk of our time as adults falls into what our bishop, Reverend Nathaniel Wilson, calls "maintenance," which is all of those mundane things that must be done in the course of our days and years to keep life moving smoothly. This includes, personal grooming, running a household, auto maintenance, job and family responsibilities, etc. Parents, do not believe the fallacy that children should not have household responsibilities at young ages. Mothers seem to be particularly susceptible to the erroneous feeling that requiring young children to do chores is cruel and unusual punishment. On the contrary, the benefits are manifold: children learn to complete tasks competently, become equipped to run their own households efficiently, feel pride and self-esteem from being significant, integral members of the family team, and learn universal lessons of

> I went by the field of the lazy man, and by the vineyard of the man devoid of understanding; and there it was, all overgrown with thorns: its surface was covered with nettles; its stone wall was broken down. When I saw it, I considered it well; I looked on it and received instruction: A little sleep, a little slumber, a little folding of the hands to rest; So shall your poverty come like a prowler, and your need like an armed man.
>
> – Proverbs 24:30-34 NKJV

perseverance, duty, and delayed gratification. As a bonus, they experience the sweet satisfaction earned when the job is done right. Don't cheat your little ones out of such valuable and rewarding lessons!

We did not mention the best benefit—spending time side-by-side with Mom or Dad. We cannot tell you the blessed conversations that have taken place with hoes in hand or side-by-side at a sink full of soap and dishes. Do not miss this hidden but golden benefit of household responsibility. Your children will rise up and call you blessed.

How?

Teaching responsibility through daily chores and duties is done in clearly defined, incremental steps. Often parents don't know where to begin, or they become frustrated with their children for not knowing something that would seem elementary. Just as often, children become frustrated and overwhelmed when their immature reasoning ability prevents them from knowing how to break complex jobs into smaller, doable tasks. When beginning to teach our children complex chores, such as deep cleaning the bathroom, we find it helpful to use books like *Speed Cleaning*, by Jeff Campbell. The author gives pictures, lists, and easy step-by-step directions for cleaning each major area of the house. Even our six-year-old can now clean the bathrooms up to our standard (well, he is still working hard to produce that elusive, streak-free shine on the mirror), and the eight-year-old is competent to wash, dry, fold or hang, and put away the family's mountain of laundry. Beginning slowly, building success upon success, and praising them for their achievements, we are actively training our children up to maturity! We are preparing them for the skills vital to successful adult life. Consider the following steps as guidelines for teaching increased responsibility and independence in "faithful and conscientious work habits."

1. Show Them—Modeling the Job

Demonstrate the new task for the child. Children retain more of what they see than what they just hear. You know the old adage: "A picture is worth a thousand words." Explain as you work through each step; don't assume that the child is aware of all the nuances of understanding the job you have gained over the years. Again, break the job into small tasks. Ask questions, checking for understanding as you go. Demonstrate the task more than once—repetition is the key to learning!

2. Help Them—Working Side-by-Side

With tool in hand, be it dish rag, mop, or shovel, let the child talk the two of you through the job. The purpose of this is twofold. First, the person who teaches is always the best student. What goes through him, sticks to him; that is, the more senses you involve in the lesson, the more he will retain. Second, with him in the lead you will be able to check for understanding. "Remember to wipe the mirror from side to side, Honey." "Let me show you again." "Great job! You've got it!" Nothing deflates the eager little worker faster than feeling that his best effort is not meeting with your approval. Do not become frustrated with immaturity. The number of times you repeat a job together greatly depends on the age and maturity of the child as well as the complexity of the job. Repeat this step until you sense mastery of the task at hand.

3. Watch Them—Reminding and Supervising

In this phase, the child has most of the information

and skills necessary to do the job independently. She has worked next to you, accepting and practicing your suggestions, and she knows what the job looks like when it is done correctly. However, because she still may need some prompting and supervising, stay close by for any further clarification or instruction.

4. Check Them—Working Independently

Children don't do what you expect, but what you inspect. By now you are confident that the child understands how to complete the job up to your standard, so you allow him to do it autonomously. When the child has completed the job, it is your responsibility to inspect and gently instruct if necessary. Be sure to end the inspection with delighted approval.

> Children don't do what you expect, but what you inspect.

5. Leave Them—Showing Initiative and Motivation

You should now have achieved every mother's dream: a child who possesses the ability to begin and thoroughly execute any duty without reminding, prompting, or threatening, and to complete it to an acceptable standard. Stand back, watch, and enjoy the fruit of your efforts. Smile approvingly as he emulates you. He will look to you for approval, so smile and give it liberally.

> The best students are teachers!

Note: A rewarding and bonding exercise is to have the independently skillful child teach a younger sibling how to properly do a job. It builds skill and confidence in the little teacher, and begins preparing them to parent their own children. The best students are teachers!

When?

So have we convinced you? You really do need to teach Junior how to make his own bed and to help clean up after breakfast. But what if Junior is only 18 months old? For what tasks could he possibly be ready? How do we determine what are age-appropriate responsibilities? One important measuring stick is the exasperation factor. Colossians 3:21 admonishes parents, "Fathers, provoke not your children to anger, lest they be discouraged." A wise parent can tell whether their child is being lazy and sly or the job is genuinely too complex for the child's level of physical and mental maturity. Go back and have the child demonstrate a task that was done below your standard to check their readiness for the task. There is nothing more discouraging for a young child than to want to please Mommy and Daddy, but to fail again and again. Our Heavenly Father never allows more to be put on us than we can bear (1 Corinthians 10:13), so we must be cautious to give responsibilities that are within the child's ability to perform successfully. *Remember,* just as every child walked and talked at different ages, so will they mature in their motor and cognitive abilities at various ages. Approach each child with love and understanding. Challenge him to grow, but do not provoke him. Following are some suggestions for age-appropriate tasks:

9-24 Months

• Putting dirty clothes in hamper.

• "Helping" with grocery shopping (putting items in basket and on check-out counter, handing things to Mom to be put away at home).

- Cleaning with Mom (give child a dust rag, child-size broom, empty spray can/Windex bottle for "pretend" cleaning).

- Watering plants (with pre-measured amounts!).

- Beginning to help make beds (begins with handing the pillows to Mom until later).

- Yard work (helping collect trash and toys, etc.).

- Following simple commands and performing errands ("bring the diaper to Mommy, please," etc.).

2-3 Years

Continue the previous responsibilities, plus the following:

- Generally including child in every-day activities on a regular basis (cleaning, shopping, etc.).

- More complicated errands ("Take this towel and put it in the hamper," etc.).

- Laundry (beginning to help with sorting by Mom handing him things to put in appropriate piles, transferring clothes from dryer to basket, etc.).

- Learning more specific neatness qualities (putting toys in proper spots).

- Taking his dishes to the sink and helping to clear the table.

- Carrying groceries in from car (give child one light item or a small bag).

- General errands (carrying diaper bag into sanctuary, carrying Mom's purse to the car, etc.).

- Putting books and magazines in a rack.

- Placing napkins, plates, and silverware on the table.

• Cleaning up what they drop after eating.

3-4 Years

Continue the previous responsibilities, plus the following:

• Making bed (begins with watching Mom—Mom helping child—Mom watching child) standards must be clear and reminders frequent.

• Keeping room neat and taking daily responsibility for it.

• Morning daily routine becoming established (getting dressed, cleaning room before breakfast).

• Learning to use the telephone properly.

• Established and regular responsibilities (cleaning bedroom, getting the mail, emptying bathroom trashcans, etc.).

• Helping wash the car.

• Simple hygiene—brush teeth, wash and dry hands and face, brush hair.

• Undress self—dress with some help.

• Carrying boxed or canned goods from the grocery sacks to the proper shelf.

4-5 Years

Continue the previous responsibilities, plus the following:

• Taking his laundry to designated place on laundry day.

• Sorting laundry with supervision.

- Begin learning to fold laundry and put it away.

- Vacuuming/sweeping.

- Cleaning table after meals.

- Helping with meal preparations (learning to measure, stir and use small appliances).

- Spreading butter on sandwiches.

- Preparing cold cereal.

- Helping Mother prepare plates of food for the family dinner.

- Making a simple dessert (add topping to cupcakes, pour the toppings on ice cream).

- Holding the hand mixer to whip potatoes or mix up a cake.

- Setting the table.

- Taking out the trash.

- Carrying groceries in from the car and putting them away.

- Helping with grocery shopping and compiling a grocery list.

- Polishing shoes and cleaning up afterwards.

- Following a schedule for feeding pets.

- Helping do the dishes or fill the dishwasher.

- Dusting the furniture.

- Helping clean out, vacuum, wash and polish car.

5-6 years

Continue the previous responsibilities, plus the following:

• Unsupervised responsibilities (making bed, washing out trashcans, etc.).

• More complicated meal preparations (making frozen juice or toast, cutting with blunt knife, baking).

• Making own sandwich or simple breakfast, then cleaning up.

• Pouring own drink.

• Preparing the dinner table.

• Tearing up lettuce for the salad.

• Helping with younger siblings (changing diapers, helping with bath, bottle feeding, entertaining while Mom is out of the room, feeding/dressing toddler siblings).

• Laundry (sorting, learning to use the washer/dryer, measuring detergent, folding clean clothes and putting them away).

• Cleaning (using cleaning supplies properly, cleaning unsupervised areas like bathtub or polishing furniture, cleaning mirrors and windows).

• Sons—carrying "heavy" things for Mom and helping with yard work.

• By this time child will begin to carry out responsibilities unasked and begin to offer help in areas in which parents don't require help.

• Making bed and cleaning room.

• Independently choosing outfit and dressing.

• Answering the telephone and beginning to dial the phone.

• Paying for small purchases.

• Helping clean out the car.

- Taking out the garbage.
- Feeding his pets and cleaning the living area.

6-7 years

Continue the previous responsibilities, plus the following:

- Simple meals prepared (making sandwiches for lunch, preparing drinks, fixing breakfast for Mom and Dad, preparing salad for dinner, peeling vegetables).
- Regular quiet time becoming a part of daily routine.
- Increased responsibilities for younger siblings (dressing infants/toddlers, entertaining them for longer periods by reading to them/playing records, etc., helping school them).
- Learning the purpose and beginning supervised usage of tools (lawn mower, hand tools, etc.) and helping with home maintenance.
- Shaking rugs.
- Watering plants and flowers.
- Preparing own school lunch.
- Helping hang clothes on the clothesline.
- Hanging up own clothes in the closet.
- Gathering wood for the fireplace.
- Raking leaves and pulling weeds.
- Keeping the garbage container clean.
- Cleaning out inside of car.
- Straightening or cleaning out silverware drawer.

- Oiling and caring for bike.

- Taking phone messages.

- Running errands for parents.

- Sweeping and washing patio area.

- Watering the lawn.

- Washing dog or cat.

- Training pets.

- Taking pets for walk.

- Carrying in grocery sacks.

- Getting self up in the morning and going to bed at night on own.

- Carrying own lunch money and notes back to school.

- Leaving the bathroom in order.

- Doing simple ironing.

8-10 years

- Continue the previous responsibilities, plus the following:

- Complete responsibility for their rooms on a daily basis (bed making, dresser drawers, closet, vacuuming, etc.).

- Unsupervised yard work (lawn mowing, edging, clean-up, gardening).

- More complex meal preparations (pouring and making tea, coffee, and instant drinks, using sharp instruments, baking, using appliances, beginning meal planning).

• More difficult cleaning projects (scrubbing kitchen floor, windows, cleaning appliances).

• Summer jobs (lawn mowing, dog sitting, babysitting, odd jobs for vacationers).

• Financial planning (computing percentages for saving, tithing, offerings, gift-giving and assuming responsibility with parental oversight).

• Beginning car maintenance (helping Dad with minor repairs, learning tool usage, washing/waxing).

• Helping rearrange furniture. Helping plan the layout.

• Running own bathwater.

• Helping others with their work when asked.

• Shopping for and selecting own clothing and shoes with parent.

• Changing from school clothes to play clothes without being told.

• Folding blankets.

• Sewing buttons and mending rips in seams.

• Cleaning storage room.

• Cleaning up animal "messes" in the yard and house.

• Cutting flowers and making a centerpiece.

• Picking fruit off trees.

• Painting fence or shelves.

• Writing thank-you notes.

• Helping with defrosting and cleaning the refrigerator.

• Feeding the baby.

- Cleaning patio furniture.

- Waxing living room furniture.

- Changing sheets and putting dirty sheets in hamper.

- Buying groceries using a list and comparative shopping.

- Receiving and answering own mail.

- Waiting on guests.

- Simple first aid.

- Doing neighborhood chores.

- Sewing, knitting, or weaving (even using a sewing machine).

- Doing chores without a reminder.

- Learning banking and to be thrifty and trustworthy.

- Handling sums of money up to $5.00.

11-12 years

Continue the previous responsibilities, plus the following:

- Putting siblings to bed and dressing them.

- Cleaning pool and pool area.

- Respecting others' property.

- Running own errands.

- Mowing lawn with supervision.

- Helping Father build things and do family errands.

- Scheduling time for studies.

- Buying own sweets or treats.

- Responsible for a paper route.

- Checking and adding oil to car under supervision.

13-15 years

Continue the previous responsibilities, plus the following:

- Could run household without supervision if necessary.

- Determine how late he should stay up during the week. Also determine how late he should be out for evening gatherings (through mutual parent-child discussion and agreement).

- Responsibility for preparing family meals.

- Social awareness: good health, exercise, necessary rest, correct weight, nutritious food, physical examinations.

- Anticipating the needs of others and initiating the appropriate action.

- Accepting both capabilities and limitations.

- Self-respect or individual worth.

- Responsibility for one's decisions. [21]

You're Bored? Great!

It is not the goal of Christian parenting to make sure that our children have fun. "Childhood is brief, so we must make it as action-packed and fun as possible for our children while they are young," is a fallacy that is gaining momentum today. "They will have to work for the rest of their lives; let's let kids be kids." Again, it is our duty and objective as Christian parents to nurture our children to a state of full development or readiness in godly intellectual, practical, moral, and spiritual training. "Hey, wait a minute," you say. "What about all that 'delight stuff'? I thought we were *supposed* to have fun." Absolutely! However, we are not to be driven to make every day "a trip to the amusement park," but to seek incidental joy and delight while on the journey to adulthood. Although fun is an important part of the process and a by-product of our attitude and actions as leaders of our families, fun itself is not the goal.

"Dad, I'm bored." "There's nothing fun to do." "Do I have to do my homework? It's sooooooo *boring*." "Can we go somewhere fun today? It's boring at home." Sound familiar? One of the plagues of this century is the fallacy that we must be constantly entertained and on the go. We heard a father give the ultimate response to such comments. "What? You're bored?" he asked with exaggerated surprise, "Terrific! Son, do you realize how much of my life as an adult is boring? You are getting some great training for your future. Isn't that terrific!" How could the child respond negatively?

As responsible adults, much of our time revolves around duty rather than pleasure. For most hard-working Americans at least eight of every twenty-four hours are spent at work, roughly one or two are spent in preparation and transportation for that job, seven or eight hours are slept away, and home, family, and health maintenance account for another few hours each day. There is very little time left for pleasure activities. There are five days of work and two for rest and play in each week. Similarly, of the fifty-two weeks in each year, most working-class people have two or possibly three weeks for vacation, while the rest are spent at the grindstone of work. When will our children learn to value and enjoy hard work? If they are conditioned to believe that their job is simply to play, at what age will they suddenly and wholeheartedly learn to work hard and love doing it? Eighteen is too late!

A Word of Caution

Habits and attitudes are caught, not taught. If we preach the intrinsic benefits of hard work to our children and then grumble about our job, we are wrong. The attitude of our heart will speak far louder than the words on our lips. Let *us* find joy in *our own* labor. If we find no joy, then we should *make some ourselves*. We can make the task a party: laugh, sing, and whistle while we work. Our enthusiasm will be contagious.

> **Habits and attitudes are caught, not taught.**

For example, our children used to dread scrubbing our rather large kitchen floor on their hands and knees. Then Kirsten began allowing them to don kneepads (the kind used with scooters or skateboards). Suddenly everyone was vying for the chance to participate in the great soap races. They begin at one side of the room on their knees, with scrub brushes in hand, and slide on suds as they fly across the room frantically scrubbing as they go. The swabby, the guy who wets the floor with the mop, directs traffic and judges the races. Is it messy at times? Yes! Would it be easier if Kirsten did it herself? Yes! Is it worth the ruckus? Absolutely! When is the last time your children begged to scrub the floors for you? Ours do! Make being responsible fun.

While our children are young we must train them in the tasks and responsibilities they will need to be adult leaders. We must, as we have explained before, train their palate to find pleasure in that which is good and godly. In this case, we want to train our children to execute thoroughly any duty at hand, without reminding, prompting or threatening, to its completion, to an acceptable standard. To be responsible is the third facet of Christian maturity.

Mottos to Work By

We have posted these sayings and reminders all over our house from time to time for years. Similar to our standards, our children immediately know what is implied if we begin quoting any of these mottos.

Use them as they appear below or modify them—they work!

Work Hard, Work Fast, Don't Stop, Ask for More…..
Do it all CHEERFULLY

———

Don't put it down, put it away

———

If it takes less than 30 seconds, do it now!

———

Duty Before Pleasure

Miscellaneous Thoughts on Household Chores

A job half done is a job undone. Do not allow work that is not up to standard. Make them re-do it. One time Adam had to sweep the kitchen floor four times before he got it right. He thought he was going to be sweeping for the rest of his life. After that episode he did a great job the first time around.

———◆———

When the children argue about whose responsibility it is to do a job, make them both do it. Have one wash the breakfast dishes, then put them back in the sink and let the other one do it. The absurdity of the quarrel becomes obvious, even funny. They won't quarrel after doing this exercise a few times.

———◆———

As with standards, written expectation as well as predetermined divisions of labor save incredible headaches. We divide chores into breakfast cleanup (two kids do this so cleanup is fast), lunch cleanup (remember we home school, and all seven of us eat lunch at home), yard and cars, and "ground zero" (which came before 9-11-01; this is living room, bathroom and other "public areas" maintenance). The duties are posted on a reusable chore chart we keep in the hall. Each job lasts one week and rotates on Monday. Everyone helps at dinnertime and has specific duties. We use this time to talk, sing, laugh and have family fellowship.

———◆———

We do not allow grumbling or complaining from a child asked to pitch in with an extra chore or to do a special favor for Mom or Dad. We expect a cheerful, "Yes, Sir, I'd be happy to" in response to a request for help. If this is not the response, we add another errand or chore. If the improper attitude is still evident, they keep getting little jobs added until they get the picture. Actually, it can become quite comical.

Teach mutual respect by not allowing children to leave a mess to be cleaned by someone else. Require them to pick up after themselves.

You Just Never Know!

A few years ago, in the middle of an average home schooling day (if there is such a thing) our phone rang. The caller announced his name in such a way that it sounded like I should have been impressed. After a pause, he explained that he was the evening news anchor of a local television station (hence the reason I hadn't recognized his name—we don't own a television). He explained that a report had come out that day that said fewer and fewer children were being required to do household chores. That morning his news team had located a family of self-described slobs who had agreed to allow the cameraman and news anchor to document their lifestyle. The newsman had then called a mutual friend, asking if she had any suggestions for a family who still required the children to do chores. He needed a family that would provide an interesting contrast for the evening news broadcast. Our friend had given him our name.

After quick consideration, we realized that, even though we had not brought a television into our home to influence us, God was giving us the opportunity to bring all of Sacramento into our home so that we could influence them! Praise the Lord!

We had exactly one hour to prepare our home and six Kings for such an honor. Thank God, we know how to work as a team. When the news crew arrived, they walked through *every room of our home,* filming as they went, opening closet doors, surveying the back yard and garage. They followed each child around while he or she did a chore, and asked each of them candid questions about how they enjoyed their responsibilities. Talk about Mama holding her breath!

Although we never had the opportunity to see the story, we received incredible feedback from those who did. We were even stopped in public a few times by people who recognized us. Friends, we tell this story, *not* to boast, but to encourage you to live for excellence!

— *Kirsten*

Seest thou a man diligent in his business? He shall stand before kings; he shall not stand before mean men (Proverbs 22:29).

Remember, Its SIMPLE...

• Remember our goal as Christian parents is to prepare our children as they develop to maturity and readiness for adult responsibilities. The second facet of responsibility is faithful and conscientious work habits.

• The benefits to conscientious work habits are manifold: children learn to complete tasks competently, become equipped to run their own households efficiently, feel pride and self-esteem from being significant, integral members of the family team, and learn universal lessons of perseverance, duty, and delayed gratification. As a bonus, they experience the sweet satisfaction earned when the job is done right.

• Teaching responsibility through daily chores and duties is done in clearly defined, incremental steps.

• It is useful to invest in books to help with housekeeping skills. Often the author gives hints, tips, pictures, lists, and easy step-by-step directions for cleaning each major area of the house.

• Consider the following steps as guidelines for teaching increased responsibility and independence in "faithful and conscientious work habits."

1. Show Them—Modeling the Job Demonstrate the new task for the child

2. Help Them—Working Side-by-Side Use patience and wisdom in direction. Correction at this point should be positive and gentle.

3. Watch Them—Reminding and Supervising The child has most of the information and skills necessary to do the job independently.

4. Check Them—Working Independently Children don't do what you expect, but what you inspect.

5. Leave Them—Showing Initiative and Motivation Stand back, watch, and enjoy the fruit of your efforts.

• *Remember,* just as every child walked and talked at different ages, so will they mature in their motor and cognitive abilities at various ages. Approach each child with love and understanding. Challenge him to grow, but do not provoke him.

• It is our duty and objective as Christian parents to nurture our children to a state of full development or readiness in godly intellectual, practical, moral, and spiritual training.

• It is not the goal of Christian parenting to make sure that our children have fun.

• Habits and attitudes are caught, not taught. If we preach the intrinsic benefits of hard work to our children and then grumble about our job, we are wrong. The attitude of our heart will speak far louder than the words on our lips. Let *us* find joy in *our own* labor. If we find no joy, then we should *make some ourselves.* We can make the task a party: laugh, sing, and whistle while we work. Our enthusiasm will be contagious.

Last Chapter
THE UN-CONCLUSION

A s young parents we were overwhelmed at the honor and responsibility of molding our angelic bundles of joy into mature, dependable, contributing members of society. We had discovered some vital things we could do to help shape our children's lives, and we also knew that to neglect these vital areas would misshape them. We looked to published experts, such as James Dobson, Gary and Ann Marie Ezzo, Michael and Debbie Pearl, Reb Bradley, Ted Tripp, Richard Fugate, and others. We carefully, prayerfully, and diligently sought out people whose worldviews matched ours and who valued a godly influence on their children. We looked to those whose children were growing and blossoming into the sort of upright, mature blessings we desired our own children to become. We were obsessed with a burning desire to give our children the best opportunity to be raised according to God's perfect design. More than one night in bed, staring into the blackness, we asked ourselves if there was something weird about us that we would be so single-minded and driven to pursue this one subject. We wondered if other young parenting couples shared a similar struggle with finding God's direction in order to make good Bible-based decisions about child rearing. In our immaturity, we did not realize that our passion for family was God-given; we talked it, read it, prayed it, and lived it. We memorized parenting and marriage Scriptures. Of course, we failed at times. Even after following godly pursuits with the purest of hearts and intents, our imperfect humanness got in the way. We grew weary in well doing and became inconsistent and frustrated. We lost our temper or became distracted. Our children sometimes did not respond the way we thought they should.

Leaning...Leaning

When we as parents come up against times of disappointment and frustration, we must not give up! The stakes are too high, and the enemy of our souls does not slumber. Those down times are when we must lean on the everlasting arm of *our Father*. We can call on Him for strength and direction, which He will faithfully supply.

Just when we thought we had this parenting thing down to a science, the Lord saw fit to humble us. There had been times when we would see a child throwing a fit in the grocery store. We would look at each other with raised eyebrows that said, 'Wow! That child is really out of control. If that mother would be consistent, she would not have to deal with such an unruly monster.' As you might foresee, we were headed for a major humbling.

God blessed us with five children, each having a unique personality and temperament. Some were sweet natured and eager to please Mommy and Daddy; they required little more than a disappointed look to bring them under control. However, one particular child presented a much greater challenge. (We will use the pronoun *he* to protect the innocent.) Before this child's birth, Kirsten was sure he would break one of her ribs, so great was his fighting instinct and forceful movement. This child crawled at four months old and seemed to break every other King family baby book record for mobility and vigor. By the time he was 13 months, we were sure that we were dealing with an entirely different temperament than our other children had exhibited.

One sunny summer morning Kirsten said, "Come to Mommy, Sweetie," expecting compliance.

The little one backed up against the wall, and with a defiant tilt of the head, strongly said, "NO."

Thinking that the little angel must not have understood her, Kirsten took the baby's hand and led him to where she had asked him to come, repeating the command as she went, "Come to Mommy." She then returned him to his spot of defiance, went back to her place (which was only four short feet away), and repeated, "Come to Mommy, Honey."

"NO," was the undeniably defiant reply.

Kirsten took the little one, swatted him and returned the tearful baby to his place. "Now, come to Mommy."

"No," he said with tears on his cheeks.

And so mother and baby began the battle of wills that lasted forty-five minutes. Recognizing that she must not let this little rebel win, Kirsten resolved to lay all of the day's demands aside until she won the contest. In tears herself, Kirsten again placed the child in his spot of defiance, only four feet from where she had called him, and said, "Honey, come to Mommy." With a scrunched up, tear stained face, he finally put up his arms and toddled to his mother. She hugged him and loved him, praising his obedience.

Again, we dug into the books, knowing that we would need all of our best artillery for the strength of will that we had just seen displayed. We were comforted by the experts' concurrence that the "strong willed child" only requires two or three such episodes to train him to comply. We read those reassuring words over and over and over for the next few years. It seemed at times that this child's sole purpose in life was to dismantle every parenting theory we had constructed. We were perplexed, exhausted, and frustrated. Although our confidence wavered at times, we stayed on our knees. We knelt daily at the couch, Bible in hand, and reminded God of His promises: "Your Word says that foolishness is bound in the heart of *my* child, but that the rod of correction will drive it far from him (Prov. 22:15). You said, 'Withhold not correction from *my* child; for if thou beatest him with the rod, he shall not die. Thou shalt beat him with the rod and deliver his soul from hell' (Prov. 23:13-14). God, you see our determined consistency with this little one. We are reminding you of your Word today. You *cannot* lie. Your Word is *true*. You *will* drive foolishness far from our child. You *will* make a champion out this child. You *are* true to your promises. We trust you."

Day after day, challenge after challenge, we held to God's promises and plan. In the process He was reshaping *us*. We no longer looked in judgment at those parents of fit-throwers in the grocery store. The roles had been reversed; now *we* were the embarrassed parents of a whirling dervish at the check stand. *We* experienced their helplessness and frustration. *We* walked, red-faced, out of the store with a 30-pound screamer over our shoulder. Our parenting ideas were challenged and strengthened, and our compassion and understanding for other parents was greatly multiplied. Now, this child's ready compliance is sweeter than the finest chocolates. We tried God's Word in the midst of the battle and it proved to be true!

The Un-Conclusion

The underlying intent in sharing the preceding story is to encourage you to trust in God and not in formulas—

no matter how powerful—to help your children become everything they can be. If we have virtuoso pianists at the age of seven, but they do not play for the glory of God, what will it profit? If our little darlings read fluently at the early age of three, four, or five, yet they do not love the timeless Word of God, what is the benefit? If they say, "Yes, sir," on cue and bring refreshments to your guests with manners that Emily Post would admire, yet they do not serve the Savior of their souls, the training has all been in vain.

In all of our doing, we must remember the highest calling as parents, and that is discipleship. Yes, we want self-controlled, wise, responsible children who grow into self-controlled, wise, and responsible adults; we have spent twelve chapters emphasizing the biblical rationale and methods to do so. We will continue "doing" with all of our might. The "doing" is un-concluding; it is daily, weekly, and yearly. But let us leave you with one overarching admonition: Let us not lose sight of the purpose of all our "doing." We are striving to raise children whose burning, driving desire is to love the Lord and to glorify Him in all that they do.

As we strive to foster self-control, we strive to create a loving atmosphere in our home. We play music that lifts up the name of Jesus. As we strive to foster wisdom, we open the Book of Wisdom ourselves, learning, growing, allowing our children to see us leaning on the everlasting Word of truth. What they know of the Savior is what we portray, and what they know of forgiveness is reflected in us. It is our responsibility and honor to create a sanctuary of love, peace, and prayer in which they can be nurtured and encouraged.

What an honor! What a journey!

Notes

[1] Webster, Noah. *An American Dictionary of the English Language.* New Haven, 1828.

[2] Bradley, Reb. *Child Training Tips.*, Fair Oaks, California: Family Ministries Publishing, 1995, p.27.

[3] Bradley, p.27.

[4] Bradley, p.27.

[5] McGerr, Patricia. "Johnny Lingo's 8-Cow Wife." June 3, 2003 <www.angelfire.com>.

[6] Bradley, p. 75-77.

[7] Bradley, p. 77-80.

[8] Lapin, Rabbi Daniel. *Thou Shall Prosper.* Hoboken, New Jersey: John Wiley & Sons, Inc, 2002, p.1.

[9] Adapted from Hildersham, Arthur. "Lectures to Mothers," 1624 as found in *Growing Kids God's Way* by Gary and Anne Marie Ezzo.

[10] Wilder, Laura Ingalls. *Farmer Boy.* New York, NY: HarperCollins, 1994.

[11] Pearl, Michael and Debi, *To Train Up a Child.* Pleasantville, TN: The Church at Cane Creek, 1994.

[12] Aaron, Raymond, "Smart Goals, Massive Results" audio cassettes. Richmond Hill, Ontario, Canada: The Monthly Mentor.

[13] Smalley, Gary and John Trent, Ph.D. *The Blessing.* New York, NY: Pocket Books, p.48.

[14] Ibid. p.89.

[15] Willats, Brian. "Breaking Up is Easy to Do." citing Statistical Abstract of the United States, 1993. American Divorce Reform. June 30, 2003 <www.divorceform.org/chilrate.html>

[16] American Medical Association, American Academy of Pediatrics, American Psychological Association, American Psychiatric Association,

American Academy of Family Physicians, American Academy of Child & Adolescent Psychiatry. "Joint Statement on The Impact of Entertainment Violence on Children Congressional Public Health Summit" July 26, 2000. June 30, 2003 <http://www.lionlamb.org/research.html>.

[17] Aiken, Jonathan and the Associated Press." Study Links Teen Drug and Alcohol Use with Promiscuity." CNN.com December 7, 1999. Cable News Network. June 30, 2003 <www.cnn.com>.

[18] National Institute on Drug Abuse." High School and Youth Trends." National Institute on Drug Abuse. June 25, 2003. National Institute on Drug Abuse, National Institute of Health, U.S. Department of Health and Human Services. June 30, 2003 <http://www.nida.nih.gov/Infofax/HSYouthtrends.html>.

[19] Bradley, p.27.

[20] Covey, Stephen. *The Seven Habits of Highly Effective People*. New York, NY: Simon and Schuster, 1989.

[21] Adapted from Author(s)." Practical Suggestions for Responsibilities You Can Expect Your Child to Begin at Specific Ages." New Life.net. **New Life Community Church of** Stafford, Virginia. October 5, 2003. <www.newlife.net>.

Works Cited

Aaron, Raymond, "Smart Goals, Massive Results" audio cassettes. Richmond Hill, Ontario, Canada: The Monthly Mentor.

Aiken, Jonathan and the Associated Press." Study Links Teen Drug and Alcohol Use with Promiscuity." CNN.com December 7, 1999. Cable News Network. June 30, 2003, <www.cnn.com>.

American Medical Association, American Academy of Pediatrics, American Psychological Association, American Psychiatric Association, American Academy of Family Physicians, American Academy of Child &Adolescent Psychiatry. "Joint Statement on The Impact of Entertainment Violence on Children Congressional Public Health Summit" July 26, 2000,

June 30, 2003, <http://www.lionlamb.org/research.html>.

Bradley, Reb. *Child Training Tips.*, Fair Oaks, California: Family Ministries Publishing, 1995.

Covey, Stephen. *The Seven Habits of Highly Effective People.* New York, NY: Simon and Schuster, 1989.

Ezzo, Gary and Anne "Marie, *Growing Kids God's Way*" audio cassettes, 1993, Hildersham, Arthur, "Lectures to Mothers," 1624. pp. 213 & 214

Lapin, Rabbi Daniel. *Thou Shall Prosper.* Hoboken Jew Jersey: John Wiley & Sons, Inc, 2002.

McGerr, Patricia. "Johnny Lingo's 8-Cow Wife." June 3, 2003 <www. angelfire.com>

National Institute on Drug Abuse." High School and Youth Trends." National Institute on Drug Abuse, June 25, 2003. National Institute on Drug Abuse,National Institute of Health, U.S. Department of Health and Human Services. June 30, 2003.< http://www.nida.nih.gov/Infofax/ HSYouthtrends.html>.

New Life Community Church Author(s)." Practical Suggestions for Responsibilities You Can Expect Your Child to Begin at Specific Ages" New Life.net. **New Life Community Church of** Stafford, Virginia. October 11, 2003. <www.newlife.net>.

Pearl, Michael and Debi, *To Train Up a Child.* Pleasantville, TN: The Church at Cane Creek, 19994.

Smalley, Gary and John Trent, Ph.D. *The Blessing.* New York, NY: Pocket Books, p.48.

Webster, Noah. *An American Dictionary of the English Language.* New Haven, 1828.

Wilder, Laura Ingalls. *Farmer Boy.* New York, NY: HarperCollins, 1994.

Willats, Brian. "Breaking Up is Easy To Do." http://www.divorceform. org/chilrate.html). Michigan Family Forum citing Statistical Abstract of the United States,. 1993.